Jane Austen

Jane Austen

A Life Revealed

CATHERINE REEF

CLARION BOOKS
Houghton Mifflin Harcourt • Boston • New York • 2011

Clarion Books
215 Park Avenue South
New York, New York 10003

Clarion Books is an imprint of Houghton Mifflin Harcourt Publishing Company.

www.hmhbooks.com

The text was set in 11-point Birka.

Library of Congress Cataloging-in-Publication Data is available.
LCCN 2011008146
ISBN 978-0-547-37021-7

Manufactured in the United States of America
DOC 10 9 8 7 6 5 4 3 2
4500310331

For Jennifer Greene

Contents

The Austen Family

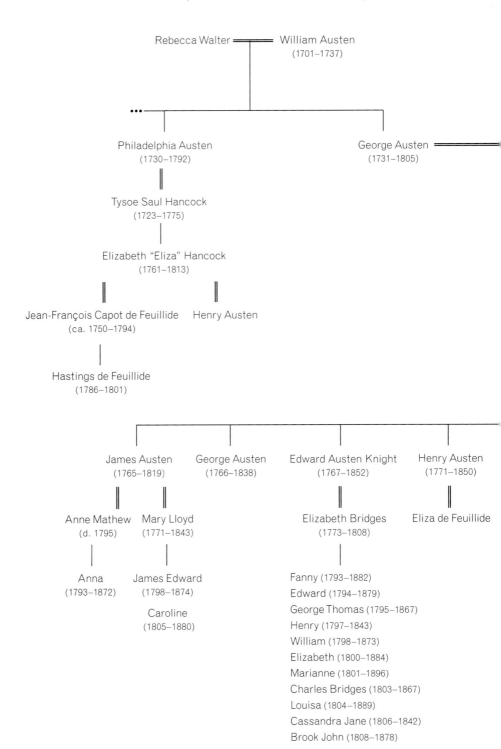

- Rebecca Walter m. William Austen (1701–1737)
  - …
  - Philadelphia Austen (1730–1792) m. Tysoe Saul Hancock (1723–1775)
    - Elizabeth "Eliza" Hancock (1761–1813) m. (1) Jean-François Capot de Feuillide (ca. 1750–1794); m. (2) Henry Austen
      - (with Jean-François Capot de Feuillide) Hastings de Feuillide (1786–1801)
  - George Austen (1731–1805) m. …
    - James Austen (1765–1819) m. (1) Anne Mathew (d. 1795); m. (2) Mary Lloyd (1771–1843)
      - (with Anne Mathew) Anna (1793–1872)
      - (with Mary Lloyd) James Edward (1798–1874)
      - (with Mary Lloyd) Caroline (1805–1880)
    - George Austen (1766–1838)
    - Edward Austen Knight (1767–1852) m. Elizabeth Bridges (1773–1808)
      - Fanny (1793–1882)
      - Edward (1794–1879)
      - George Thomas (1795–1867)
      - Henry (1797–1843)
      - William (1798–1873)
      - Elizabeth (1800–1884)
      - Marianne (1801–1896)
      - Charles Bridges (1803–1867)
      - Louisa (1804–1889)
      - Cassandra Jane (1806–1842)
      - Brook John (1808–1878)
    - Henry Austen (1771–1850) m. Eliza de Feuillide

The Leigh Family

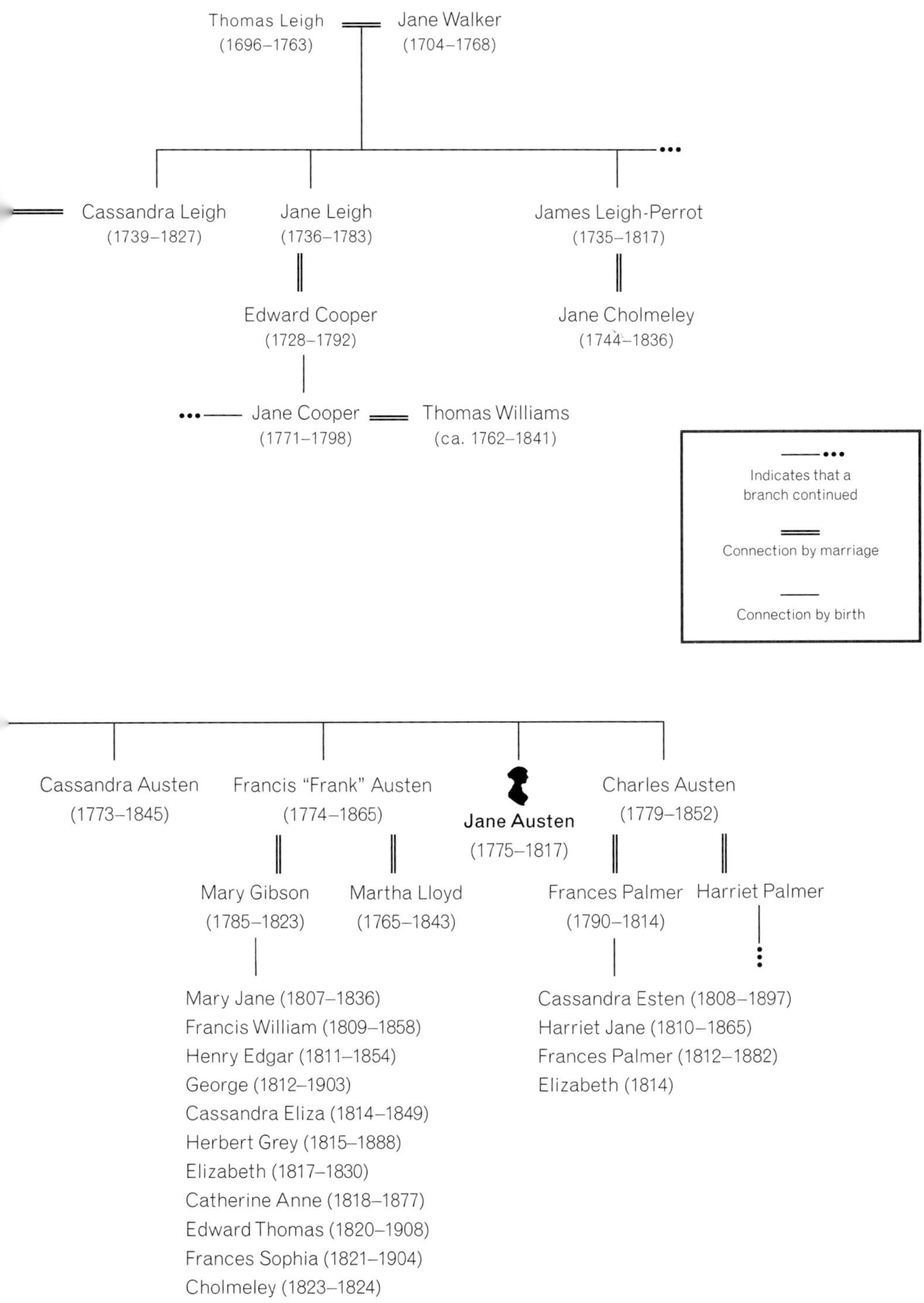
Thomas Leigh (1696–1763)
Jane Walker (1704–1768)
Cassandra Leigh (1739–1827)
Jane Leigh (1736–1783)
James Leigh-Perrot (1735–1817)
Edward Cooper (1728–1792)
Jane Cholmeley (1744–1836)
Jane Cooper (1771–1798)
Thomas Williams (ca. 1762–1841)
Indicates that a branch continued
Connection by marriage
Connection by birth
Cassandra Austen (1773–1845)
Francis "Frank" Austen (1774–1865)
Jane Austen (1775–1817)
Charles Austen (1779–1852)
Mary Gibson (1785–1823)
Martha Lloyd (1765–1843)
Frances Palmer (1790–1814)
Harriet Palmer
Mary Jane (1807–1836)
Francis William (1809–1858)
Henry Edgar (1811–1854)
George (1812–1903)
Cassandra Eliza (1814–1849)
Herbert Grey (1815–1888)
Elizabeth (1817–1830)
Catherine Anne (1818–1877)
Edward Thomas (1820–1908)
Frances Sophia (1821–1904)
Cholmeley (1823–1824)
Cassandra Esten (1808–1897)
Harriet Jane (1810–1865)
Frances Palmer (1812–1882)
Elizabeth (1814)

I cannot anyhow continue to find people agreable.

—Jane Austen, May 13, 1801

one

GENTLE AUNT JANE?

Now be sincere; did you admire me for my impertinence?

—Pride and Prejudice

Charlotte Heywood, twenty-two, has grown up healthy, useful, and obliging. Away from home for the first time, she waits in a sitting room at Sanditon House to be greeted by her hostess, the twice-widowed Lady Denham. It is early in the nineteenth century, and as Charlotte waits, she ponders. Why does a large, full-length portrait of Lady Denham's second husband hang above the mantelpiece? In contrast, the great lady's first husband, Mr. Hollis—the man who built Sanditon House—is portrayed in a miniature that would fit in Charlotte's palm. And what is being said just then by Lady Denham's nephew, Sir Edward, to the penniless Clara

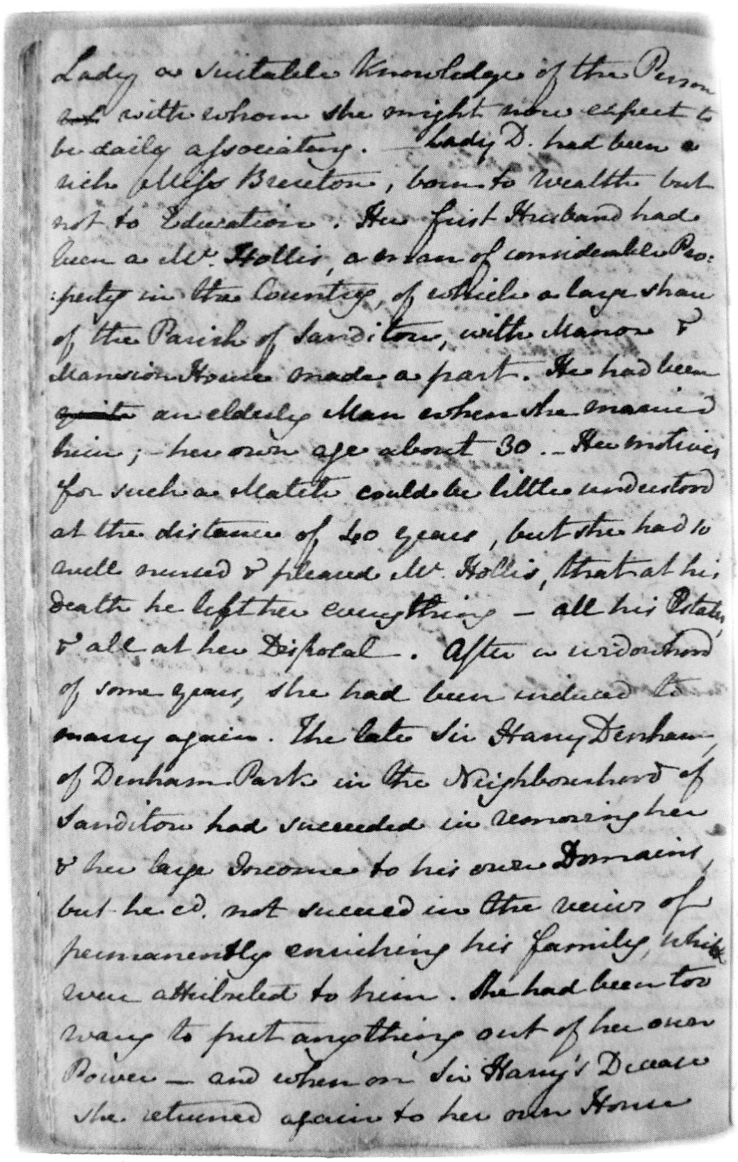
Lady a suitable Knowledge of the Persons
~~and~~ with whom she might now expect to
be daily associating. — Lady D. had been a
rich Miss Brereton, born to Wealth but
not to Education. Her first Husband had
been a Mr. Hollis, a man of considerable Pro:
:perty in the Country, of which a large share
of the Parish of Sanditon, with Manor &
Mansion House made a part. He had been
~~quite~~ an elderly Man when she married
him; — her own age about 30. — Her motives
for such a Match could be little understood
at the distance of 40 years, but she had so
well nursed & pleased Mr. Hollis, that at his
death he left her everything — all his Estates,
& all at her Disposal. After a widowhood
of some years, she had been induced to
marry again. The late Sir Harry Denham,
of Denham Park in the Neighbourhood of
Sanditon had succeeded in removing her
& her large Income to his own Domains,
but he cd. not succeed in the views of
permanently enriching his family, which
were attributed to him. She had been too
wary to put anything out of her own
Power — and when on Sir Harry's Decease
she returned again to her own House

Most of Jane Austen's handwritten manuscripts have been lost, but her unfinished last novel is one that survives. Austen called this story *The Brothers,* but after her death, her family changed its title to *Sanditon*.

Brereton? Charlotte glimpsed the secret lovers outdoors, holding a private conversation, as she traveled up the broad, handsome approach to Sanditon House . . .

Then Jane Austen's characters fell under a spell. When Austen put down her pen on March 18, 1817, too ill to add another word to her story, she made time stand still for Charlotte and the others. For two centuries, not a clock has ticked in Lady Denham's mansion or in the surrounding town; not a speck of dust has fallen there. Charlotte Heywood waits and wonders, her eyes focused on the tiny portrait of Mr. Hollis, never blinking. Lady Denham stands frozen in place, one foot raised, poised to enter the sitting room. Clara and her suitor sit motionless, side by side forevermore.

How Austen would have finished her last novel, *Sanditon,* remains a mystery, one of several that confound the fans of this much-loved author. Millions of people throughout the world read and enjoy Austen's books; she and her novels are the subjects of countless films and adaptations; but very little is known about the woman herself. What did she look like? Did she have "fine naturally curling hair, neither light nor dark," as one of her many nieces recalled, or "long, long black hair down to her knees," as another niece remembered? A cousin once dubbed Austen and her sister, Cassandra, "two of the prettiest girls in England," but a niece wrote that Austen fell short "of being a decidedly handsome woman." Jane Austen died before photography was invented. The only picture of her that survives is a watercolor by Cassandra Austen, but

Cassandra Austen painted the only authenticated portrait of her sister, Jane. People who knew Jane Austen said that she bore little resemblance to this wary, unsmiling woman.

people who knew the author claimed it was a poor likeness.

No one knows Jane Austen's views on religion or politics, or even what she did or thought for weeks or months at a time. Old diaries and letters can reveal much about famous people of the past, but Austen left no diaries. After she died, her relatives destroyed many of her letters for reasons that can only be guessed. Were they too personal? Might they have hurt people's feelings, or revealed a side of Jane Austen that her family hoped to hide?

Because her novels were published anonymously, when she died at age forty-one, readers were only just starting to learn that this country clergyman's daughter—this retiring spinster—had authored *Sense and Sensibility, Pride and Prejudice,* and other popular novels that probe the human heart. Her family described Jane Austen to the world as they wanted her remembered. "Her sweetness of temper never failed. She was ever considerate," wrote her nephew James Edward Austen-Leigh. "Faultless herself, as nearly as human nature can be, she always sought, in the faults of others, something to excuse, to forgive or forget," wrote her brother Henry. Added one of her nieces, "I do not suppose she ever in her life said a sharp thing."

Not ever? It is hard to believe that such a sweet, forgiving creature would write lines such as these:

> *I do not want People to be very agreable, as it saves me the trouble of liking them a great deal.*
>
> *For what do we live, but to make sport for our neighbours, and laugh at them in our turn?*
>
> *Mrs. Allen was one of that numerous class of females, whose society can raise no other emotion than surprise at there being any men in the world who could like them well enough to marry them.*

Jane Austen's wit and cutting remarks on human nature make her novels fun to read.

Austen lived and wrote as the 1700s came to a close and a new century began. Novels were still a fairly new form of literature, made popular in England by writers like Daniel Defoe and Henry Fielding. In 1719, Defoe wrote about a shipwrecked traveler surviving on an island in *Robinson Crusoe*. In 1749, Fielding entertained readers with the bawdy, comic adventures of a young man forced to make his way in the world in *Tom Jones*. In the early 1800s, Sir Walter Scott began drawing on his-

A ship wrecks off the coast of Madagascar in Daniel Defoe's book *The Adventures of Robert Drury* (1807). Readers in Jane Austen's time savored tales of danger in faraway places.

tory to write exciting novels like *Ivanhoe* and *Rob Roy,* books filled with romance, jousting, and the storming of castles.

These authors packed their novels with action. They transported their characters to exotic locales and had them escape mortal danger with barely moments to spare. They painted on big canvases, but Austen sketched on a "little bit (two inches wide) of Ivory," she said, working "with so fine a Brush." She wrote about the kind of people she knew well, ladies and gentlemen of the English countryside, and she confined her plots to family life, friendship, courtship, and marriage. She offered readers "little touches of human truth, little glimpses of steady vision, little masterstrokes of imagination," said the American-born novelist Henry James.

Jane Austen began writing stories as a child growing up in her father's parsonage. She honed and polished her work, and in 1811, when she was thirty-five years old, her first published novel appeared. *Sense and Sensibility* offers a cynical view of a society in which money matters more than character, and in which the people who get along best know how to hide their feelings. Like all of Austen's novels, *Sense and Sensibility* concerns itself with women of marriageable age and their quest to settle happily with suitable husbands.

More novels followed, among them the sprightly *Pride and Prejudice,* in which smart, outspoken Elizabeth Bennet teaches handsome, wealthy Fitzwilliam Darcy to overcome his haughtiness as she learns to love him; *Emma,* which chronicles a year in a country village during which Emma Woodhouse gains the maturity needed to marry the right man; and *Persuasion,* in which Austen's oldest heroine gets a second chance at love.

Austen wrote in plain language and concentrated on character. Her novels reveal a deep understanding of psychology, of how people thought, behaved, and expressed themselves. Although she wrote about women and men of her own time and place, her characters still ring true, because she captured the essence of human nature.

A twenty-first-century reader who begins a Jane Austen novel enters a distant world where money and lineage made some people better than others. Marriage often boiled down to economics: for many people, choosing the right husband or

Keira Knightley and Matthew Macfadyen portrayed Elizabeth Bennet and Fitzwilliam Darcy in the 2005 film *Pride and Prejudice*. These two characters are destined to fall in love despite their initial dislike of each other.

The softly draping garments seen in ancient Greek and Roman art inspired the graceful, flowing women's fashions of Jane Austen's time. Many women chose muslin, a finely woven cotton, for their dresses, and they preferred white and pale shades to dark, somber colors. Dresses had high waists and low necklines, and sleeves often extended past the elbow. This illustration is from a fashion magazine published in 1800.

wife had more to do with gaining an income than with love. Women faced limited options. Marriage gave them social and financial security, with or without romantic love, but it carried the burden of constant childbearing and rearing. A single woman with no income had little freedom, because she depended on her family for shelter and support. Those who were qualified could teach or care for the children of others, but teaching was hard work that paid little, and governesses held a low social rank. "Single Women have a dreadful propensity for being poor," Austen wrote.

Jane Austen belonged to this world and to a big, sprawling family. She had almost no schooling and never ventured out of a small section of England. She inhabited a narrow niche, but she found in it a wealth of inspiration for her fiction. To her, gathering characters and watching them mingle became "the delight of my life," she said. "3 or 4 Families in a Country Village is the very thing to work on."

two

THE NOVELIST IS BORN

My conduct must tell you how I have been brought up. I am no judge of it myself.

—The Watsons

"Last night the time came, and without a great deal of warning, everything was soon happily over," wrote the Reverend George Austen on December 17, 1775. The night before, his wife had safely given birth to the couple's seventh child, Jane. Her father called her "a present plaything for her sister Cassy, and a future companion." He baptized her in the Church of St. Nicholas at Steventon, where he preached every Sunday.

The baby thrived, like all the sturdy Austen children, starting with James, the oldest. He was considered the writer in the family. Handsome Edward was easy to like, and gangling

Henry learned early how to use his natural charm. Cassy—Cassandra—would be Jane's closest friend and companion, making their father's prediction come true. And little Frank had a mind of his own.

George, the second boy, was healthy, too, but he had epilepsy and was deaf and slow to learn. He lived nearby, with paid caretakers who treated him kindly. No one knows how common it was for the disabled to live apart from their families. Generally, history remembers developmentally disabled people from Jane Austen's time only if they were poor. This is because their neighbors paid for their care, and their names became part of the parish record. Families like the Austens, who had a large enough income, supported their disabled members, whether these people lived at home or with others.

Children's voices filled the parsonage at Steventon, where the Austens lived, and young feet thundered up and down the stairs. As if seven children were not enough, the Reverend Austen ran a boarding school for boys. From August until Christmas, and again from February through June, pupils slept in the garret and mastered Latin and classical Greek in the parlor below. When not teaching, Jane's father wrote weekly sermons, ministered to the people of Steventon and nearby Deane, and oversaw Cheesedown Farm, in the northern part of the parish. Selling the farm's bounty, like teaching, brought in needed money.

His wife, Cassandra Leigh Austen, worked hard, too. She cared for her children, cooked meals, and washed clothing and

Jane Austen's childhood home, the Steventon parsonage, was torn down in 1828.

bed linens for her family and the pupils. She tended the kitchen garden, milked the cows, fed the chickens, collected their eggs, and sewed the family's clothes. She had a quick mind and composed poems for her children and her husband's pupils to enjoy, and she played the piano. Mrs. Austen may have been a humble clergyman's wife, but she was distantly related to nobility. She was proud of her aristocratic nose, with its bump high on the bridge and pointed tip.

The Reverend George Austen was "a profound scholar" and a man "possessed of a most exquisite taste in every species of literature," wrote one of his sons. He read aloud to his children, and once they could read to themselves, he let them choose freely from the hundreds of books shelved in his study. He owned a microscope that let him see the pearly eyes of in-

The Reverend George Austen had an active mind and encouraged his sons and daughters to read.

sects, the "animalcules" living in a drop of water, and other minute wonders of God's creation.

English people of the 1700s believed that nature revealed the power and wisdom of the Almighty. They also believed that God had placed kings and queens above dukes, earls, and viscounts. Titled nobles in turn were superior to the gentry—the refined, educated class to which the Austens belonged. The social order was so complex that different levels existed even among the gentry. Being knighted, having a prominent surname, or owning land that had been in the family for generations placed someone in the highest tier. At lower levels were bishops, smaller landowners, military officers, physicians, and clergymen like Jane's father, who were educated but had relatively little money. The upper classes and the landowning gentry looked down on people who took money in exchange for goods and services, no matter how much wealth they accrued.

The nobility and gentry took pride in their manners, which had been drilled into them almost from birth. An elaborate code of etiquette governed every social interaction, however trivial. It dictated how ladies and gentlemen entered a dining room for dinner, who spoke first when people were introduced, and where a lady might walk and with whom. Displaying proper manners to everyone, regardless of station, showed "good breeding," or a solid upbringing. Yet these arbitrary rules had another purpose as well. They "seem to have no object but exclusiveness," commented a nineteenth-century writer. In other words, they separated "good society," to whom they were second nature, from the newly rich, who had mastered them imperfectly.

The rules of inheritance further complicated the system. In Jane Austen's time, the oldest son generally inherited everything from his parents. If a family had no sons, then the estate went to the male relative next in line, possibly a nephew. This custom protected estates from being divided up, but it forced younger sons to seek their own fortune, perhaps to become clergymen or military officers. It also excluded daughters, forcing many to rely on the men in their families for support.

Men who had made fortunes in industry strived to acquire land and titles, hoping to distance themselves from common merchants and tradespeople. Luckily for them, it was not impossible to gain admission to a higher social circle. There were plenty of families among the upper classes who were short of cash and eager to acquire it.

Two children from a family of gentry give a coin to a beggar in this painting from 1793. Like all children of their class beyond the age of three or four, the brother and sister are dressed like adults. The beggar boy, who depends on charity, lacks a hat and shoes.

Marrying a woman from a wealthy manufacturing family could make life easier for a gentleman with financial worries. The connection would also raise the status of the woman's family, allowing everyone to gain. Of course, some people ignored the rules and married for love, for better or worse.

If the poor were part of English society, then this was God's will, too. Every community had its population of people in want: laborers who had grown too old or sick to work, widows, and orphans. The law required each parish to look after its needy. Citizens were charged a tax, called the "poor rate," which bought food and firewood for the poor and paid their rent, medical bills, and burial costs. The parish found work for the able-bodied and bound poor youths as apprentices so they could learn a trade. Christians had a solemn duty to help the poor. Jane Austen knew the impoverished people living in the humble cottages of Steventon, and like all the ladies in her social circle, she gave them clothing, blankets, and other things they needed.

Steventon, with its rolling hills and winding lanes, was in the county of Hampshire, in southern England. Other places offered more beautiful views, but Steventon was known for its charming hedgerows. These borders of trees and undergrowth defined meadows, gardens, and property lines. They sheltered nesting birds, spring wildflowers, and benches for strolling ladies who stopped to rest. Steventon was in the country, but nightly carriages brought mail and passengers to and from London.

Sometimes carriages brought guests. In May 1779, the

Austens had a visit from Thomas Knight, a wealthy cousin of George Austen, and his wife, Catherine. Enchanted by young Edward's good looks and friendly ways, the Knights invited the boy to join them on their summer travels. Edward's parents, who were soon to have another child, permitted him to go. They consented again several years later, when the childless Knights offered to adopt Edward and make him their heir. Thomas Knight had a responsibility to take care of the property he had inherited and pass it along to a worthy successor. He also felt obligated to prevent his family line from dying out. He achieved both goals by adopting Edward. For the Austens, the chance for Edward to inherit a large estate was too great to pass up. The adoption took place when Edward was sixteen. It meant that he would live with the Knights at Godmersham Park, their splendid house in the county of Kent, and change his name to Knight one day. He would remain close to the family at Steventon, though.

Charles, the baby of the Austen family, was born in June 1779. Two weeks later, fourteen-year-old James left home to enter St. John's College in the city of Oxford. He had received a scholarship because his mother was distantly related to the college's founder, Sir Thomas White. James was young, but not unusually young, for someone starting college. Boys had been known to go to Oxford as early as age twelve, and James's own father had entered St. John's College in the year he turned sixteen. There was no standard system of education in James's day, so students went to Oxford when they were academically ready.

This silhouette commemorates the formal presentation of Edward Austen to the family of Thomas Knight, his adoptive father. Silhouettes, either painted or cut from paper, were a popular way to record events and make portraits before the invention of photography.

James came home for holidays, and at Christmas 1782, when Jane was just seven years old, he put on a play with his brothers and their friends the Fowle boys. The English people of Jane Austen's time loved anything to do with the stage. More plays were written in England in the 1700s than in any other century. Thousands of men and women flocked to Drury Lane, Covent Garden, and London's other popular theaters. People read plays for entertainment, and they acted them out at home for fun.

Jane Austen lived in the Georgian period, which lasted from 1714 until 1830. During these years, four kings named

A crowd cheers the actors at the Drury Lane Theatre, one of London's leading playhouses, in 1821.

George—George I, George II, George III, and George IV—sat on the English throne. England rose to be a world power, despite losing its North American colonies. It was a fruitful time, when Defoe, Fielding, Scott—and Austen—gave the world their novels. George Frideric Handel, who adopted England as his home, composed the *Messiah* and other great pieces of music. The British people of this period are referred to as Georgians.

That Christmas, James and the other boys performed *Matilda*, a rip-roaring drama set during the long-ago reign of William the Conqueror, when knights did battle in armor and "Tilts and Tournaments call'd forth the Brave." Brothers Edwin and Morcar duel for the beautiful Matilda, whom Morcar holds prisoner.

Neighbors gathered in the Austens' barn to see the play. As the other actors took their places on the stage, Edward stepped forward to recite a prologue written by James. The actors hoped, he said,

To speak with elegance, & act with ease,
To fill the softened soul with grief sincere
And draw from Pity's eye the tender tear.

Soon afterward, in 1783, their parents scraped up the money needed to send Jane and Cassandra away to school. At seven, Jane was really too young to leave home, but she insisted on doing whatever ten-year-old Cassandra did. As her mother explained, "If Cassandra's head had been going to be cut off, then Jane would have her's [sic] cut off too."

Parents who enrolled their daughters in school wanted them to come home "accomplished." Boys studied classical languages, history, mathematics, and science. Girls learned a little grammar and geography, but mostly they practiced penmanship and other ladylike skills. Women who could paint or do needlework filled empty hours and beautified their homes. Those who spoke French and knew how to dance or play an instrument mingled well in society.

Many people agreed with Jonathan Swift, who wrote that "reading books, except those of devotion or housewifery, is apt to turn a woman's brain." She would "learn scholastic words [and] make herself ridiculous by pronouncing them wrong, and applying them absurdly in all companies." Swift was a master of satire who often created humor by exaggerating popular opinions.

No laws required children to go to school, and none governed the operation of schools. Any woman needing to earn a living could open a boarding school for girls. Some of these schools were good, but others seemed designed to halt children's growth and ruin their health. Schoolmistresses who feared poverty fed their pupils meager meals of the cheapest food they could buy. Girls in their care slept two to a bed, which spread disease, and they rarely played outdoors. (Of course, life was brutal at some boys' schools as well.)

It is hard to understand why caring parents would send their children to such dreadful places. Most likely, many fathers and mothers had no idea how terrible conditions were. But people believed that hardship was good for children, that it toughened them and made them better fit for life.

Jane, Cassandra, and their cousin Jane Cooper went to a school run by a woman named Mrs. Cawley, in her Oxford home. When summer came, Mrs. Cawley took her pupils to the southern port of Southampton, just as a "putrid fever"—possibly typhoid or diphtheria—spread through that city. Jane, Cassandra, and Jane Cooper all fell ill. For a time their parents thought that everything was fine, because Mrs. Cawley had forbidden the girls to send letters home. Then plucky Jane

Cooper disobeyed and sneaked out a letter to her mother—possibly saving her cousin Jane's life by doing so. Mrs. Cooper and her sister, Mrs. Austen, hurried to Southampton to find Jane Austen on the brink of death.

The little girl improved under her mother's constant care, and as soon as she was well enough to travel, the two women took their daughters home. But Mrs. Cooper had been infected, and she died soon afterward. From then on, Jane Cooper was often at Steventon.

The three girls briefly attended a better school, beginning in 1785. At least the pupils played outdoors, and there was plenty of bread and butter for breakfast. The headmistress, an Englishwoman who called herself Madame La Tournelle, hurried through her pupils' lessons so that she could talk to them about her favorite subject, actors. Jane, Jane Cooper, and Cassandra returned to Steventon in 1786 and had no more formal education. As young as she was, Jane Austen had seen enough

Jane Austen's mother, Cassandra Leigh Austen, shows off her noble profile. After her sister's death, she gave motherly attention to her niece Jane Cooper.

of girls' schools to form a strong dislike of them, and she never changed her mind. She later described them as places "where young ladies for enormous pay might be screwed out of health and into vanity." At home, she read freely, and her parents hired a piano master to give her lessons. Playing the piano became one of Jane Austen's accomplishments, one that would give her pleasure throughout life.

Being home meant being on hand when the boys put on more plays. These shows were most fun to watch when captivating Cousin Eliza joined the cast. Eliza was the daughter of Aunt Philadelphia, the Reverend Austen's older sister, who as a young woman had sailed to India in search of a husband. English wives were in demand among the men employed by the British East India Company, the large firm that traded for Asian goods. Philadelphia Austen married Tysoe Hancock, the company surgeon, in 1753, and Eliza was born in 1761.

Hancock died when Eliza was thirteen, and from then on her godfather looked after her welfare. Warren Hastings, governor general of Bengal, was a powerful man in India. He was a rich one, too, and placed ten thousand pounds in trust for the fatherless girl. This was a large sum of money in the eighteenth century. The Reverend Austen earned a couple of hundred pounds a year, at most, as a clergyman. He, in turn, was much better off than a teacher in a London charity school, who received thirty-six pounds a year and lodging, or a serving man, who felt lucky to get twenty pounds plus room and board.

Philadelphia Hancock took Eliza to France, where they attended balls with the king and queen, Louis XVI and Marie Antoinette. At nineteen, Eliza married a French nobleman, Count Jean-François Capot de Feuillide. The count was attracted to Eliza's income as well as her charms, because he needed cash for a big project, draining the swamplands on his estate. He greatly admired England, so when Eliza became pregnant, he decided that the child should be born on English soil and grow up as a native of the British Isles. He, of course, was too busy with his drainage scheme to make the trip. So, "notwithstanding my reluctance to quitting home in my present situation, & my still greater regret at separation from the Comte [Count] de feuillide at a period when I could the most have wished for his presence, I purpose setting out on this long projected journey," Eliza wrote to an English cousin.

Eliza traveled to England with her mother for the birth, but the baby arrived early, in June 1786, before the women reached their destination. Eliza named the boy Hastings, for the godfather who had treated her so generously. She was in England in 1789, when the French Revolution began.

Although fond of both Austen sisters, Eliza confessed that "still My Heart gives the preference to Jane." Jane admired this grown-up cousin who wore French fashions, flirted playfully with Henry and James, and was so knowing and accomplished. Eliza broadened the younger girl's world by telling her about France and the famous people she had met there. She encouraged Jane to read French with a gift of children's books printed in that language. When she sat at the piano and played, she taught Jane to love music as she did.

Eliza resembled characters in the many novels Jane devoured. "If a book is well written, I always find it too short," Jane wrote. As a child, she was already honing her taste in books. She found a lifelong favorite when she read *Sir Charles Grandison,* a hefty novel by Samuel Richardson. *Sir Charles Grandison* is an epistolary novel, one written in the form of letters. It tells of a virtuous gentleman torn between his love for an English heiress and his obligation to marry an Italian noblewoman. Jane read and reread Richardson's book, and she even wrote a play based on it. Years later, a nephew recalled that "every circumstance narrated in *Sir Charles Grandison,* all that was ever said or done . . . was familiar to her."

Cecilia, by Fanny Burney, was another popular novel that Jane liked. It follows the adventures of Cecilia Beverley, age twenty-one. In order to receive an inheritance, Cecilia must marry a man who agrees to take her name. This stipulation causes all kinds of upset, leading one character to commit suicide and another to have a stroke. Cecilia, meanwhile, loses most of her money to creditors and becomes temporarily insane. "The whole of this unfortunate business," a character concludes, "has been the result of PRIDE and PREJUDICE."

A number of women were writing novels and plays. Some, like Fanny Burney, looked with humor at the way English aristocrats lived. Hannah Cowley wrote lighthearted plays in which lovers scheme and surmount obstacles to marry happily in the end. Ann Radcliffe's gothic novels, filled with decaying castles, ghostly touches, and heroines in danger, kept young women of the upper and middle classes from falling asleep at night. Jane discovered spirited, realistic female characters in *Belinda* and other novels by Maria Edgeworth. She encountered a hero and heroine ruled by abundant feeling, or sensibility, in Charlotte Turner Smith's *Celestina*.

It was one thing for a woman to pursue writing as an accomplishment and another for her to see her name in print. Some women boldly signed their names to their writing, but many people thought that a proper lady avoided public attention. Mary Brunton, who published her novel *Self-Control* anonymously, preferred to "glide through the world unknown" rather than "be suspected of literary airs." Brunton said, "I would sooner exhibit as a rope-dancer" than be known as the author of a book.

Then there was the feminist writer Mary Wollstonecraft, who took credit for a controversial book, *A Vindication of the Rights of Woman.* "The minds of women are enfeebled by false refinement," Wollstonecraft wrote; women "are treated as a kind of subordinate beings, and not as a part of the human species." The nonconforming Wollstonecraft had famous men as lovers, bore a child out of wedlock, and married an outspoken atheist. She stirred debate about whether women should write for publication and what they should write if they did.

Young Jane Austen knew what she liked in a novel, and she

laughed at what she deplored. When James and Henry briefly published a journal called *The Loiterer,* they received a humorous letter from a female reader calling herself "Sophia Sentiment." Miss Sentiment had written to complain, because the stories in *The Loiterer* contained "not one Eastern Tale full of Bashas [pashas, or Turkish officials] and Hermits, Pyramids and Mosques." One particular story had "no love, and no lady in it, at least no young lady." She asked to see "some nice affecting stories, relating to the misfortunes of two lovers, who died suddenly, just as they were going to church." There is no proof, but some scholars think Sophia Sentiment was thirteen-year-old Jane Austen.

Jane also wrote stories of her own. She dedicated one, *Love and Freindship* (Austen's spelling), to Eliza de Feuillide. This brief epistolary novel finds dark humor in carriage crashes, thievery, and elopements. Its two heroines, Laura and Sophia, are constantly fainting, until Sophia swoons once too often and falls on the dewy grass, catching a fatal chill. "Beware of fainting-fits," she warns her friend. "Though at the time they may be refreshing and agreable, yet believe me they will, in the end, if too often repeated and at improper seasons, prove destructive to your constitution."

Written in 1790, when she was fourteen, *Love and Freindship* is one of Jane Austen's early works, which together are called the Juvenilia. Between roughly 1787, when she was eleven, and 1793, the year she turned eighteen, Austen composed stories, dramatic scenes, short novels, and an imagina-

Mary

This woman had the good luck of being
anced to the throne of England, inspite
the superior pretensions, Merit, & Beauty
er Cousins Mary Queen of Scotland & Jane
y. Nor can I pity the Kingdom for
misfortunes they experienced during
Reign, since they fully deserved them,
having allowed her to succeed her Brother
ich was a double piece of folly, since they
ht have foreseen that as she died without
dren, she would be succee

disgrace to humanity, that pest of society, Eliza-
-beth. Many were the people who fell Martyrs
to the protestant Religion during her reign;
I suppose not fewer than a dozen. She mar
-ried Philip King of Spain who in her Sister's
reign was famous for building Armadas. She died
without issue, & then the dreadful moment came
in which the destroyer of all comfort, the deceitful
Betrayer of trust reposed in her, & the Murderess of
her Cousin succeeded to the Throne. —
Elizabeth

Mary

This woman had th
advanced to the throne of

Cassandra illustrated one of Jane's juvenile works, "The History of England."

tive account of the history of England. She copied the ones she liked best into three slender notebooks. Writing to entertain her family, the young Jane Austen made fun of social customs and the startling events that happened all too often in novels.

Already she was setting herself apart from society and acting as an ironic observer.

An older cousin, another woman with the odd name Philadelphia, noticed young Jane taking on airs. Philadelphia Walter, who was as sweet as vinegar, met the Austen girls in 1788, when they visited relatives in the southeastern county of Kent. Watching Jane across a dinner table, Walter saw a girl who appeared "not at all pretty & very prim," as well as "whimsical & affected." Jane, a bright adolescent, was showing off her cleverness in company. Walter preferred Cassandra and called her pretty. She saw a strong resemblance between Cassandra and herself, but Cassandra, Walter noted, "was not so well pleased with the comparison."

Jane set another short novel, *Jack and Alice,* in the village of Pammydiddle. This fictional place is home to drunkards, gamblers, and "envious, spiteful, and malicious" young women. It was also home to wealthy Charles Adams, a man "of so dazzling a beauty that none but eagles could look him in the face." Adams sets a steel trap to catch by the leg any woman who approaches his house with marriage on her mind.

The young author dedicated *Jack and Alice* to "Francis William Austen Esqr"—her brother Frank. A graduate of the Royal Naval Academy at Portsmouth, Frank sailed to the East Indies at fourteen on the frigate *Perseverance.* He would spend five years away from his family. In his parting words to his son, the Reverend Austen reminded Frank that his behavior toward others would affect his success: "You may either by a con-

Jane Austen's oldest brother, James, followed his father into the church.

temptuous, unkind and selfish manner create disgust and dislike; or by affability, good humour and compliance, become the object of esteem and affection."

As Frank set sail, the other Austen brothers were getting on with their lives. Charles followed Frank into the naval school. James completed his studies and became a clergyman, like his father. In March 1792, he married beautiful Anne Mathew, the daughter of a general who gave her a yearly allowance of one hundred pounds. The newlyweds settled into the parsonage at Deane, where James took over the churchly duties. Their daughter, Anna, was born in April 1793. In later years, Mrs. Austen liked to tell of being called from her bed in the middle of the night and trudging to Deane through the early spring mud to help deliver her granddaughter.

Edward married, too. His bride, Elizabeth Bridges, was a baronet's daughter. Edward lacked a title, but he was going to inherit wealth, mostly in the form of land and houses. For this reason, he made a good match for Elizabeth. Edward and Elizabeth also had a child in 1793, a girl named Fanny. Henry Austen grew to be more than six feet tall and started college in Oxford on a founder's scholarship, like James. His parents wanted him to be a clergyman, too, but in February 1793, England went to war with France. Henry left college and rushed to join the Oxford militia. By early 1794, he was guarding French prisoners at Portsmouth. "Oh, what a Henry!" was all Jane could say about this impulsive brother.

Life offered less adventure to the Austen girls. Around December 1792 Cassandra became engaged to Tom Fowle, one of the boys who had acted in plays at Steventon. It would be a long time until the couple could afford to marry, because Tom was a minister in a poor parish, and Cassandra had no money.

Daydreaming about her own future, Jane made fanciful entries in her father's church register. She recorded the unions of "Henry Frederic Howard Fitzwilliam of London and Jane Austen of Steventon," "Edmund Arthur William Mortimer of Liverpool and Jane Austen of Steventon," and "Jack Smith and Jane Smith late Austen, in the presence of Jack Smith, Jane Smith." The easygoing Reverend Austen never crossed out these entries. They remain part of the record of parish weddings, christenings, and deaths.

three

LOVE AND LOSSES

I am almost afraid to tell you how my Irish friend and I behaved.

—letter to Cassandra Austen, January 9, 1796

JANE AUSTEN frustrates anyone who tries to catch a glimpse of her. She seems to turn away or slip behind a hedgerow as soon as an observer draws near. A curious reader can only imagine what she looked like, based on the brief descriptions that have survived—even if these contradict one another.

By October 1792, at age sixteen, Jane was "greatly improved as well in Manners as in Person," from the way she appeared to Philadelphia Walter in 1788, according to Eliza de Feuillide.

One of the Fowle brothers compared her to a doll, because she had a bright expression and "a good deal of color in her face." Then he changed his mind and said she was really more

This silhouette, discovered in an early edition of Austen's novel *Mansfield Park,* bears the inscription *"L'aimable Jane"* ("The amiable Jane"). Art experts at Britain's National Portrait Gallery think that the woman in profile is probably Jane Austen.

like a child: "very lively & full of humor." A neighbor remembered her as "a tall thin *spare* person with very high cheek bones," whose face displayed "great colour—sparkling Eyes not large but joyous & intelligent." Others recalled that she had a round face and "full round cheeks." Some people called her eyes dark, but the family said they were hazel, like her father's. Witnesses agreed, though, that she was tall: "tall & slight, but not drooping"; "rather tall and slender, her step light and firm."

That light, firm step made her a good dancer. "She was fond of dancing, and excelled in it," Henry Austen said. Dancing was a popular social activity in eighteenth-century England. Men and women chose partners for the fashionable dances of Jane Austen's youth, but couples danced in groups. They performed "figures," or sets of movements, like those in American square dancing. They might step toward each other and back, join hands and circle, or cross from one position to another. Men and women formed two opposing lines for one of the liveliest and best-loved country dances, the Sir Roger de Coverley. Couples doing this dance took turns stepping forward to perform their fanciest figures and then danced their way to the ends of the lines.

Good manners required a couple to enjoy one or two dances together and then separate and pair up with others. And gentlemen took care that every lady wishing to dance was invited onto the floor. Someone, usually an older married woman, provided music on a piano.

Country gentlefolk perform "lumps of pudding," a popular dance.

The Austens gathered socially with the families of clergymen, lawyers, doctors, and landowning gentlemen who had no need to work. The Bigg family, consisting of a widower with several children, lived in a nearby manor house called Manydown. Three of the Bigg daughters—Catherine, Elizabeth, and Alethea—were Jane and Cassandra's friends.

The Austen girls counted Martha and Mary Lloyd among their friends as well. Martha and Mary lived with their mother, a clergyman's widow. Mary Lloyd and Jane Austen were nearly the same age, but Jane preferred Martha, who was ten years older and had a sense of humor. Mary Lloyd had survived the dreaded smallpox, which killed 400,000 Europeans every year in the 1700s. Most of the deaths occurred in cities like London, where people lived packed together and smallpox was a constant threat. In 1779, a typical year, smallpox killed twenty-five hundred Londoners. Every so often an epidemic erupted, and smallpox spilled into the countryside, infecting and killing people there.

There was nothing to be done for people who caught smallpox except pray that they survived. Painful blisters burst out on their skin, often covering every bit of the face. Their skin felt as if it were on fire and sometimes came off in sheets. This evil disease tortured the body's surface without mercy, but it did its worst damage inside, attacking the throat, lungs, intestines, liver, and other organs. Smallpox had left Mary's face badly scarred, but she was lucky to have escaped the blindness and other disabilities that were common among survivors. No one in Jane Austen's lifetime knew that a virus caused smallpox, but those who blamed it on "animated atoms" were on the right track.

The Lloyds and the Fowles were cousins, and Martha and Mary's sister had married one of the Fowle brothers. The Georgians approved of marriage between first cousins, because it kept money and property within a family.

The Austens' social circle also included the Lefroys. The Reverend George Lefroy, his wife, Anne, and their three young children occupied the rectory in Ashe, the village beyond Deane. Anne Lefroy wrote poetry, and she encouraged younger writers, including Jane Austen. She was a great reader who could recite Shakespeare's verses from memory.

At Christmas in 1795, the Lefroys had a visit from their nephew. Tom Lefroy was nearly twenty and had grown up in Ireland. Blond, handsome, and smart, he was soon headed for London, to study law. He met Jane Austen when the Biggs hosted a holiday ball at Manydown and hung lanterns in their greenhouse to illuminate the night. Immediately, Tom and Jane felt drawn to each other, and they seemed not to care who knew it.

Society expected correct, dignified behavior from a woman who had reached the age for marriage. A young, single woman was to be chaperoned in public at all times, and she was to speak to a gentleman only if he had been properly introduced. She could write to him only if they were engaged, and she knew never to be alone with him. Jane and Tom skirted the rules of decorum, attracting the attention of their elders.

Cassandra Austen missed the shameful display, because she was staying with the Fowles in Berkshire, but Jane told her all about it in a letter. Twenty-year-old Jane asked her sister to imagine "everything most profligate and shocking in the way of dancing and sitting down together." Jane and her "Irish friend" had met three times, but already Tom Lefroy was being teased about her. They would see each other again before he left Hampshire, at a ball hosted by his aunt and uncle in the rectory at Ashe.

This letter to Cassandra, dated January 9, 1796, is the earliest piece of Jane Austen's correspondence that escaped destruction. It reveals a carefree young woman joyously in love who believes herself loved in return. She passes along news of friends and family but keeps returning to the subject most on her mind: Tom Lefroy. His jacket is too light in color, she writes, but this is because he admires Tom Jones, the hero of Henry Fielding's novel, who wore white when he was wounded.

Jane was just as buoyant five days later, when she wrote to Cassandra again. This time, she confided that she expected to receive an offer of marriage during the ball at Ashe. "I shall refuse him, however," she joked, "unless he promises to give away his white coat."

The proposal never came, though. Tom's family had big plans for him, and they did not include marrying a penniless girl. The son of an army officer, Tom needed a wife who would bring wealth to the match. Her money would allow him to live in an affluent style and make friends who could help him get ahead. The Lefroys noticed the budding romance and nipped it early by hurrying Tom off to London. Jane never saw or heard from him again.

How she bore up—whether she cried, went without sleep, and let the world see her sorrow—cannot be known. The next letter that Cassandra spared from the flames was written seven months later, in August, when Jane's feelings were under control.

Jane dared not ask anyone about Tom Lefroy, but she listened closely when her father did. During a visit to the Steventon parsonage in November 1798, Anne Lefroy told the Reverend Austen that Tom had finished his studies in London and was returning to Ireland. Within a year he married an Irish heiress, with whom he would have a big family. He went on to serve in Parliament, and in 1852 he was named lord chief justice of Ireland, which was then under English rule. He might possibly have enjoyed the same success with Jane as his wife, but it would have been much harder to achieve. In old age Tom Lefroy admitted that he was once in love with Jane Austen, but he said it had been a "boyish love."

Anne Lefroy introduced Jane to another man in 1797. The Reverend Samuel Blackall, a graduate of Emmanuel College in Cambridge, expected to be appointed to a good parish soon. He liked company and conversation, and he was at an age to marry. Who could be a more suitable mate than the smart daughter of a fellow clergyman? No one knows how the meet-

Thomas Langlois Lefroy, who carried on a brief youthful romance with Jane Austen, served as chief justice of the Court of Queen's Bench in Ireland, retiring at age ninety.

ing went, but in 1798 Blackall wrote to Anne Lefroy that he looked forward to seeing the Austens again. He had "the hope of creating to myself a nearer interest." But, he added, "at present I cannot indulge any expectation of it." His words imply that Jane had been blind to his charms. If Anne had hoped to make a new match for Jane, to atone for the one her family had prevented, the plan failed.

Jane's comments back this up. After seeing Blackall's letter, she wrote with relief to Cassandra, who was staying with Edward at Godmersham, that the marriage-minded minister would not be visiting the Lefroys. "And it is therefore most probable that our indifference will soon be mutual, unless his regard, which appeared to spring from knowing nothing of me at first, is best supported by never seeing me." Anne Lefroy had little to say about the matter. Jane wrote: "Perhaps she thinks she has said too much already."

When Austen learned much later that Blackall had finally married, she recalled him mockingly as "a piece of Perfection, noisy Perfection himself." His wife, she said, would need "to be of a silent turn & rather ignorant, but naturally intelligent and wishing to learn."

Other people might divert love's course in real life, but novelists can devise happy endings. Jane Austen's heroines would marry their chosen suitors, despite differences in income and class. By the time she met Tom Lefroy, Austen had begun a novel in letters called *Elinor and Marianne.* It focused on two sisters, one who relies on caution and good sense, and another who follows her heart. In October 1796, she began another novel, *First Impressions,* which featured a family of modest means with a flock of daughters nearing the age for marriage.

First Impressions delighted Jane's family and friends. Martha Lloyd read it so many times that Jane playfully accused her of scheming to memorize it and publish it herself. The Reverend Austen thought it was good enough to be printed. He sent his daughter's manuscript to a distinguished London publisher, Thomas Cadell, without revealing the author's name. Cadell thought less of the novel than the author's proud father did, however. He scrawled across the top "Declined by Return of Post" and sent it back to Steventon.

The novels Jane Austen wrote in her twenties were longer than the Juvenilia. As an adolescent she had imagined characters who behaved badly and had placed them in ridiculous circumstances. Even *Lady Susan,* a novel-length work written when she was eighteen, featured a heroine whose heart was so cold that she forgot she had a daughter. This was all quite amusing, but as Austen grew into adulthood, she sought greater challenges as a writer. She began creating characters with the ambitions, talents, fears, and quirks of real human beings. She placed them in realistic situations that revealed their flaws and tested their strengths. She was learning to apply her wit sparingly, but with greater effect. A dedicated writer, she wrote steadily, even in times of grief.

Sorrow visited Austen and her family on a regular basis. Too often in the late eighteenth century, sickness and accidents snatched away people who only a short time before had been young and full of health. One day in 1795, Anne Austen, James's wife, felt ill after eating dinner. Within hours, she was dead, the cause of her death a mystery. Little Anna went to live with her grandparents and aunts at the parsonage in Steventon.

When Jane Cooper fell in love with Captain Thomas Williams of the Royal Navy, her happiness seemed certain. The couple soon married, with Jane and Cassandra Austen serving as witnesses. In 1796, when her husband was knighted for commanding a ship that helped capture two French vessels, Jane Cooper Williams became Lady Williams. Two years later, she was driving a two-wheeled carriage, enjoying the scenery on the Isle of Wight, off England's southern coast, when she collided with a runaway workhorse. She was thrown to the ground and killed.

Misfortune targeted Cassandra Austen, too. At the close of 1795, her Tom—Tom Fowle—joined the army. He was to be chaplain in a regiment that was sailing to the West Indies to fight the French. Military service would take him away from England for more than a year, but Lord Craven, the nobleman in charge of the regiment, had promised to place him in a thriving parish after the war. Fowle's reward would be a decent income and the chance to marry much sooner.

Cassandra expected Tom Fowle to return in spring 1797, but "alas instead of his arrival news were received of his death." Fowle had died of yellow fever in February, and the news had taken three months to reach England. "Jane says that her sister

Cassandra Austen gave up all thoughts of marriage at age twenty-four, upon learning that her fiancé had died.

behaves with a degree of resolution & propriety which no common mind could evince in so trying a situation." The person describing Cassandra's strength is not Jane, who was at her sister's side, but Eliza, whose information was secondhand. Any letters that Jane might have written about this unhappy time were later torn up and tossed into a fire.

Lord Craven swore that he never would have let the young minister sail to such a disease-ridden place if he had known about the engagement. His words failed to comfort Cassandra, though. Twenty-four and beautiful, she decided never to marry. She put on the cloth cap and high collar of a middle-aged woman and hurried into spinsterhood.

No one weathered more storms, however, than Eliza de Feuillide. Early in 1791, her mother, Jane's aunt Philadelphia Hancock, discovered a lump in her breast. It was the first sign of the cancer that would kill her. Eliza hoped for "the unspeakable happiness of seeing my beloved parent restored to Health," but Hancock looked forward to pain, illness, and certain death. The only remedies to be had were quack cures, and one of these gave temporary relief. By the end of the year, she needed laudanum, a drug made from opium, to dull her pain, and she died in February 1792.

"Poor Eliza must be left at last friendless and alone," predicted her sourpuss cousin, Philadelphia Walter. "The gay and dissipated life she has long had so plentiful a share of has not ensur'd her friends among the worthy: on the contrary many who otherwise have regarded her have blamed her conduct & will now resign her acquaintance."

Eliza confounded those small minds that gloated over her bad fortune. Her friends stayed loyal, and her husband came from France to be with her in her grief and, at long last, meet his son. He had to hurry home, because France threatened to seize his property if he stayed away too long, but he hoped to

Philadelphia Hancock enjoyed a more adventurous life than most Englishwomen of her time, living in both India and France.

return to England soon. Eliza fought off melancholy and did her duty, as she saw it.

She doted on her son, but she worried about him, too. Little Hastings was sickly, and he suffered frequent, violent seizures that damaged his brain. When most children his age learned to talk, Hastings made noises but said no words. While they took their first steps, he had to be carried. He would learn to walk and talk only with great effort. There would be no paid caretakers for Hastings, though. Eliza kept the "dear little Boy" close to her and gave him the very best care that she could. She took him to seaside spas, hoping that ocean bathing and salty air would build his strength.

Meanwhile, the count faced danger as a nobleman in France. The French Revolution had given way to the bloody Reign of Terror. After abolishing the monarchy, France's new leaders saw enemies everywhere: in neighboring nations and states, within the Roman Catholic Church, and especially among the nobility. They beheaded thousands of real or imagined traitors, including the queen, Marie Antoinette, who was executed on October 14, 1793. Neighboring peasants attacked Eliza's husband and laid waste to his estate, but he survived. By February 1794 he was in Paris, where he tried through bribery to free an aged noblewoman from jail. He was promptly arrested, put on trial, and sentenced to death. The count lost his head on the guillotine on February 22, 1794.

A proper waiting period elapsed before Henry Austen asked Eliza to marry him in 1795, but she turned him down. A year later, the widowed James Austen also proposed marriage to her, and she refused him, too. She hated to give up "dear Liberty, & yet dearer flirtation," she said. But liberty could be lonely, so when Henry renewed his proposal, Eliza said yes. Henry earned a steady income as an army captain, and Eliza knew "the excellence of his Heart, Temper, and Understanding." Henry cared for Eliza, but more important to her was "his Affection for my little Boy." It hardly mattered to Eliza—or anyone else—that she was ten years older than her husband-to-be. When she and Henry married in 1797, the Reverend Austen sent forty pounds to Henry's regiment to pay for a celebration.

Clergyman James still wanted a wife, so he offered his hand to Mary Lloyd, the smallpox survivor. She accepted, and this couple also married in 1797, on a snowy day. The match thrilled Mrs. Austen, who told Mary that if the matter had been up to her, "you, my dear Mary, are the person I should have chosen for *James's wife, Anna's Mother,* and *my Daughter.*" She felt sure that Mary would "greatly increase & promote the happiness of each of the three."

Jane Austen thought that Mary lacked a warm and giving heart and could never like her. And although Eliza praised her as "very sensible & good-humoured," Mary hated Eliza, who laughed and enjoyed life, regardless of what it held in store. Wearing stylish dresses and hats, and spoiling her tiny dog, Eliza drew the eyes of many men. Mary could hardly forget that this French-speaking cousin had been her husband's first choice. She made it clear that Eliza was never welcome in her home.

Mary found it hard to love her stepdaughter as well. Four-year-old Anna went to live with her father and Mary, but she missed life at Steventon, especially happy times spent in the sitting room that her aunts shared. A grown-up Anna described this room, remembering fondly "the common-looking carpet with its chocolate ground that covered the floor," and a painted press—a cabinet for storing clothes—with bookshelves above. In her mind Anna saw her aunt Jane's pianoforte and her aunts' twin sewing boxes, decorated with inlaid wood, which sat on a table between two windows.

The woman in this 1809 cartoon walks on pattens to protect her shoes and skirt from the mud.

Jane and Cassandra often walked from Steventon to Deane, to drop in on Anna and her family. On sloppy days they wore pattens, platforms attached to their shoes to lift them above the muddy lane. Anna liked to watch her approaching aunts, two best friends who wore identical bonnets. "I made it a pleasure to guess, & I believe I always guessed right, which bonnet & which Aunt belonged to each other," she said.

Anna had a half brother before the nineteenth century began. James Edward Austen was born in 1798. By that year, Edward and Elizabeth Austen had five children and looked forward to more. Edward had gained possession of Godmersham Park, the Knights' great estate, and much of their other property.

Jane's parents had closed their school in 1796. By then the Reverend Austen's hair had grown white, and his wife had lost her front teeth, but both remained healthy and longed to see new sights. A chance came in May 1799, when Edward and Elizabeth invited twenty-three-year-old Jane and her mother to travel with them to the resort town of Bath.

four

UPROOTED

I consider everybody as having a right to marry
once in their Lives for Love, if they can.
—Letter to Cassandra Austen, December 27, 1808

HOW THE Georgians loved Bath! The health-conscious drank the water that bubbled from its hot springs, believing it cured their ills. Edward Austen complained about poor digestion and hoped the water would bring him relief. Many single women went to Bath for another reason: to snag a husband out of the crowd that strolled around the pump room, where the wonder-working water was dispensed. Jane Austen's own mother and her aunt Cooper had both met their husbands in Bath.

Tourists in this growing city had plenty to do. Bath offered public gardens, Roman ruins, dances, concerts, and plays featuring actors from the London stage. People with ailments real or imagined could consult the many doctors who had offices there. Mrs. Austen's well-off brother, James Leigh-Perrot, who suffered from gout, traveled often to Bath with his wife. (James Leigh became James Leigh-Perrot when he inherited the fortune of a great-uncle named Perrot.) Mrs. Austen had taught her offspring to treat the Leigh-Perrots with respect. The wealthy couple had no children, and she hoped they would leave their money to hers.

The Leigh-Perrots were to become minor celebrities in Bath. In August 1799, one of the city's shopkeepers caught Jane's aunt leaving his store with lace that she had not bought. Mrs. Leigh-Perrot was arrested and taken to prison. A crime like this was serious under England's strict sentencing laws. A guilty

Invalids hoping to be cured line up for spring water in the pump room.

A cartoon from 1796 lampoons the fashions on display in Bath, especially hats with long feathers for women.

verdict carried a sentence of transport to Australia or death by hanging. Jane's aunt claimed that she had been tricked, that a clerk had placed the lace in her parcel while she was looking at something else. She accused him of trying to blackmail her.

It was useless to protest, though. She remained under lock and key for eight months, first in the local prison and then in the prison keeper's dirty, noisy home, awaiting trial. In a letter from Steventon, Jane and Cassandra volunteered to show their support by attending the trial, but their rich aunt turned them down. "To have two Young Creatures gazed at in a public Court would cut one to the very heart," she insisted.

Two thousand curious spectators packed the courthouse on the day of the trial. Those hoping for a good show went home disappointed, because the jury deliberated for just fifteen minutes before declaring the defendant not guilty. (Mrs. Leigh-Perrot went free, but was she truly innocent? A few years later, a girl spotted her trying to sneak a plant out of a gardening shop without paying. Such a rich woman had no need to steal, but logic cannot always explain human behavior.)

In Bath, Jane and her mother occupied "two very nice sized rooms, with dirty Quilts and everything comfortable," Jane said. They joined their relatives to see the sights, but Jane found little to like about Bath. She joked that an outdoor concert would "have more than [its] usual charm with me, as the Gardens are large enough for me to get pretty well beyond the reach of its sound." Outdoor music at Bath was not renowned for its high quality and held no appeal for a dedicated musician like Jane Austen. She was still having piano lessons in 1796, the year she turned twenty-one. George Chard, an organist at Winchester Cathedral, traveled the roughly fourteen miles between Winchester and Steventon to instruct her.

Nevertheless, Jane made mental notes of everything she saw and heard. She was planning another novel, one set in Bath. It was going to be a humorous story about a girl with a busy imagination who reads gothic novels. The writing had to wait, though, because when it was time to leave Bath, Mrs. Austen decided to do more traveling. She wanted to visit cousins and an old friend in the counties of Gloucestershire and Surrey. And she expected Jane to come along.

With the visits over at last, life settled down and Jane returned to her writing. She added pages to the novel set in Bath, which she called *Susan,* and she rewrote *Elinor and Marianne.* She rejected the epistolary, novel-in-letters form that she had first chosen for this story. She wrote it instead as a straightforward narrative, in paragraphs and chapters. The new approach freed her to tell a broader tale, focusing on a larger cast of characters. An epistolary novel can relate only what the letter writers have to say. The new form allowed the author to speak up, to insert her own thoughts from time to time. Austen also changed the novel's title to *Sense and Sensibility.*

She took a break from writing in November 1800 to attend a ball, escorted by her brother Charles. The next day, Jane wrote to Cassandra, who was at Godmersham Park, giving her the latest gossip. One woman at the ball, Mrs. Blount, "appeared exactly as she did in September," Jane wrote, "with the same broad face, diamond bandeau, white shoes, pink husband, & fat neck." Another person, a Mr. Warren, was "ugly enough; uglier even than his cousin John." Jane had been polite to two women she called the Debary sisters, as polite "as their bad breath would allow me." Jane's jokes had sharp edges, but she saw much more than she reported to Cassandra. Every ball or social call offered lessons in human character to an observant novelist.

Cassandra was away from home, helping Edward's wife, who was having her sixth child. The baby girl was named Elizabeth, like her mother. Cassandra would be gone for a long time; she was to stay at Godmersham until February and then make a brief stop in London before returning to Steventon.

Jane, meanwhile, visited Martha Lloyd, who had moved with her mother to Ibthorpe, twenty miles away. She came home before Cassandra, at the end of November, bringing Martha with her. As the two friends entered the parsonage, Jane's parents announced that they had reached some decisions while "the girls" were away. Their father, who was nearly seventy, was retiring, and James was taking over as minister at Steventon. This meant that James and his family would live in the parsonage. The Reverend Austen, his wife—and their two unmarried daughters—were moving to Bath. The news came as a complete surprise to Jane. Her parents had given no clue that they were even thinking of such a plan. Stunned by this series of blows, Jane fainted.

The heroines of *Love and Freindship* were always swooning, but not Jane Austen. For her to faint meant that she was deeply upset. People today can only imagine the anguish she felt about losing her lifelong home and being forced to change her daily routine. She was a single woman without money of her own, so others controlled the course of her life.

Anyone would assume that Jane wrote to Cassandra right away, to pass along the shocking news and pour out her feelings. Maybe she did, but no such letter survived. If Jane wrote one, then Cassandra tore it up. In fact, no letters from Jane to Cassandra Austen are known to exist from the entire month of December 1800.

The first letter written after this catastrophe that Cassandra spared is from January 1801. By then Jane had begun to

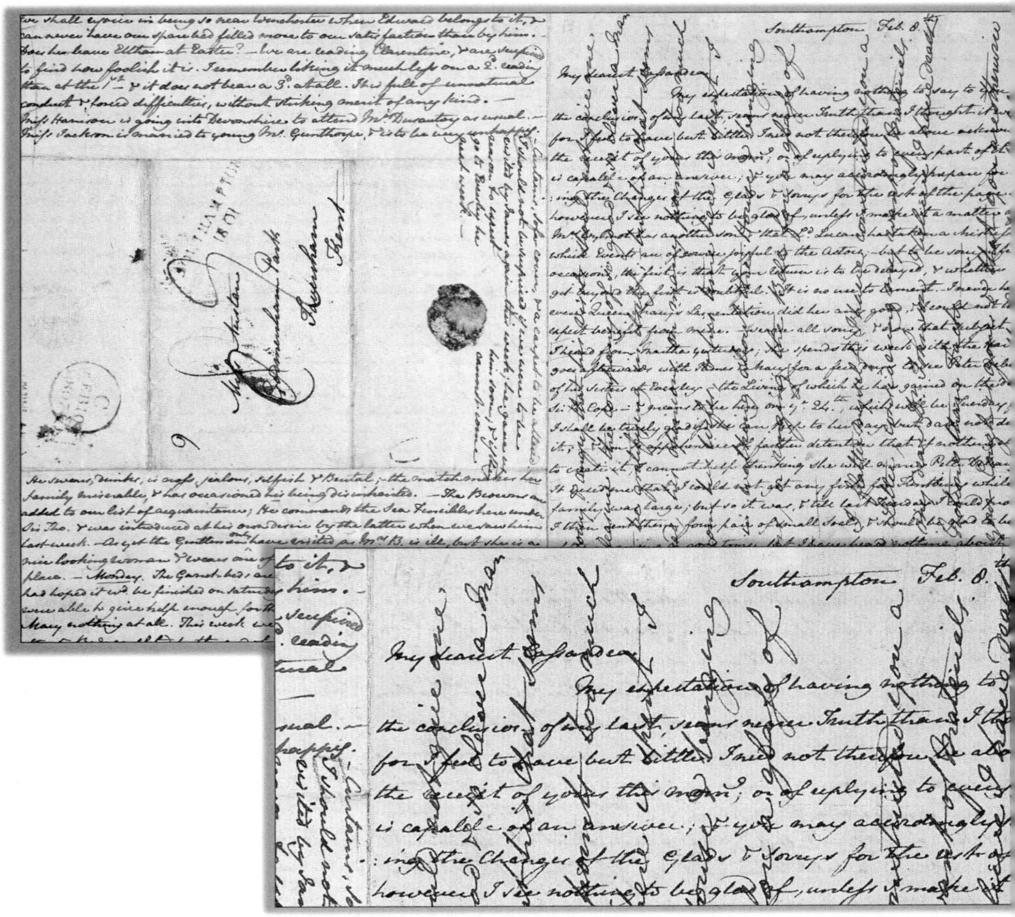

To save postage and paper, nineteenth-century letter writers squeezed as much news as they could onto every page. One common method was called cross-hatching. After filling all the space, the writer gave the paper a quarter turn and wrote over the previous lines, but in a different direction. Jane Austen employed cross-hatching in this 1807 letter to Cassandra.

accept the fact that the move would take place. She told Cassandra that she had no regrets about leaving the village of Steventon or its people. "We have lived long enough in this Neighbourhood," she wrote. Also, being in Bath would make it easier to travel to seaside towns for the summer holidays.

It made her sad, though, to see the family's possessions sold. The Austens parted with everything from farm equipment to furniture, including Jane's piano. They sold many of her father's books and even the painted scenery from the plays that the children had performed. The pictures hanging on the wall would stay where they were and become the property of James and Mary.

"The whole World is in a conspiracy to enrich one part of our family at the expence of another," Jane wrote to Cassandra. This was what bothered her most: James and Mary seemed all too eager to take over the parsonage, and the Reverend and Mrs. Austen appeared all too willing to help them. Her father's brown mare was to be James's when he moved to Steventon, but the animal "has not had the patience to wait for that, & has settled herself even now at Deane," Jane remarked. "Everything else I suppose will be seized by degrees in the same manner."

Someone made the mistake of hinting that Jane might offer her cabinet to James's daughter, Anna, the little girl who had lived at the parsonage until she was four. Jane complained to Cassandra, "as I do not chuse to have Generosity dictated to me, I shall not resolve on giving my Cabinet to Anna till the first thought of it has been my own."

The Austens' home in Bath was modern and new. From their tall drawing-room windows, Jane, Cassandra, and their parents could see the Sydney Gardens, a spot that the royal family liked to visit. They could walk easily into the center of town. Still, Jane was far from happy. She summed up Bath as "vapour, shadow, smoke & confusion," and she griped about having to attend "stupid" parties. She had to be nice to too many people, including a Miss Langley, who was "like any other short girl, with a broad nose and wide mouth, fashionable dress, and exposed bosom."

Over the next few summers, Jane, Cassandra, and their parents traveled to resort towns like Teignmouth and Dawlish, on the English Channel. Along the coast of Wales, Jane waded in the sea. She used a bathing machine, a wheeled carriage that was propelled into the water, usually by horse power. A lady

Bathing machines changed little between the early 1800s, when Jane Austen vacationed at the seashore, and the early 1900s, when this photograph was taken. Ladies emerged from the "machine" after it was pulled into the water and swam in privacy, protecting their modesty.

A steep wall protects the town from high seas at Lyme, a place Jane Austen loved.

could then open the bathing-machine door and step into the sea, safe from the eyes of gentlemen. Jane especially loved Lyme, where white, barren cliffs surrounded the coastal town, and a high seawall protected land and people alike from being washed away during storms.

The Austens made the acquaintance of other summer travelers. Many years later, Cassandra Austen reminisced about meeting a gentleman when the family traveled to the Devonshire coast in 1801 or 1802. This man and Jane formed an attachment, and when the time came to part, he asked where the Austens planned to travel the following year. Cassandra understood that he hoped to see them again. She expected him to propose marriage to Jane, and she thought that her sister was inclined to accept him. Not long afterward, however, they learned that the gentleman had died.

No one knows her lover's identity, but a historical mystery appeals to people's imaginations. In his 2009 book *Jane Austen: An Unrequited Love,* author Andrew Norman suggests that this obscure suitor was the Reverend Samuel Blackall, the man Austen met through the efforts of Anne Lefroy. Norman's theory is intriguing, but some key facts contradict it. For example, the mystery man was said to have died soon after the meeting, but Blackall lived until 1842. Until researchers find solid clues to his identity, the lover must remain unnamed.

For the Reverend and Mrs. Austen, these years of travel were "the short Holyday of their married life," said their granddaughter Anna. A handsome man in old age, the Reverend George Austen attracted notice wherever he went. His snowy hair formed soft, glossy curls over his ears and was his finest feature.

Jane and Cassandra also made visits throughout the year. The country gentry commonly stayed with relatives and friends for weeks at a time. People who were not employed could spend long stretches away from home, keeping their friends and loved ones company. This was fortunate, because traveling involved hardship and danger. Mud, holes, and stones in the road slowed the progress of horse-drawn coaches. Bad roads caused vehicles to tip over and injure passengers, sometimes fatally. Riders' purses were at risk, too, with highwaymen roaming the countryside. These bandits thought nothing of stopping a coach and robbing the passengers of their valuables.

Visiting gave single men and women time to meet potential mates and possibly become engaged. It gave social climbers a chance to connect with richer and more powerful people. For a number of reasons, it was wise to make a few long visits instead of many short ones.

A gentleman with a large estate, like Edward Knight, saw hospitality as a duty. Henry Austen often stayed at Edward's home, Godmersham Park. Henry was a welcome guest, because he knew how to please. Calling Godmersham "the Temple of Delight," he brightened holiday celebrations and children's games. Henry had left the army to become a banker, with offices in London and Hampshire.

He visited Godmersham sometimes with Eliza and sometimes alone. His stepson, Hastings de Feuillide, had died in 1801, at age fifteen. "So awful a dissolution of a near & tender tie must ever be a severe shock, and my mind was already weakened by witnessing the sad variety and long series of pain

When staying at Edward's estate, Godmersham Park, Austen enjoyed luxuries she could not afford at home.

Austen's brother Edward Knight wears clothing typical of an English country gentleman. His long cloth coat is simply styled and in a solid color. His shirt is ruffled at the collar and cuffs, and his legs are covered by close-fitting britches and long socks. By the early 1800s, the rich brocades and powdered wigs of the previous century had fallen out of fashion.

which the dear sufferer underwent," Eliza wrote at the time. She hoped that Hastings had exchanged "a most painful existence for a blissful immortality." Eliza's precious son was buried beside his grandmother Philadelphia Hancock.

The Austen sisters made several trips to Godmersham Park during their years in Bath. In Edward's great house, Jane could call for food whenever she was hungry and sip fine French wine with dinner. She could seat herself in one of the twenty-eight chairs that furnished the library and read for hours, warmed by two fires. On pleasant days, she walked the paths that wound through Edward's vast grounds, pausing to take in the beauty of walled gardens or clusters of trees that sheltered small game.

Cassandra was a more frequent guest at Godmersham than was Jane. She helped Edward's wife, Elizabeth, whenever a new baby came, and Elizabeth simply preferred her to Jane. Jane clearly was the most gifted woman in the family, and her "accomplishments" may have aroused her sister-in-law's jealousy. "A little talent went a long way" with Elizabeth, Anna Austen observed, "& *much* must have gone a long way too far."

Edward and Elizabeth's oldest daughter, Fanny Knight, saw something else: Her aunt Jane "was not so *refined* as she ought to have been from her *talent.*" She explained that "Both the Aunts were brought up in the most complete ignorance of the World & its ways (I mean as to fashion &c)." Still, "Aunt Jane was too clever not to put aside all possible signs of 'commonness' . . . & teach herself to be more refined."

Or perhaps Jane Austen flaunted her country ways and well-worn dresses. She had a low opinion of the Knights' genteel friends. "They came, and they sat, and they went," she commented. She befriended the family's governess, Anne Sharp, in whom she found a woman like herself: smart, single, and lacking money. Anne Sharp was clever enough to write a play that the children performed for the servants, called *Pride Punished or Innocence Rewarded.*

A governess held a lonely, awkward place in her employers' home. She had belonged to their social class until financial need forced her to take a paid position. Yet her education and past connections placed her above the servants in status. She was often on duty from early in the morning until the children fell asleep at night, every day of the week. Before going to bed, she had to help with the family's sewing, which left her no time to herself. For all this, she earned a small salary. A governess endured "years of chilly solitude through which the heart is kept shivering upon a diet that can never sufficiently warm it," concluded one nineteenth-century writer.

In 1802, as winter drew near, Jane and Cassandra visited their friends the Bigg sisters. Alethea, Catherine, and Elizabeth had a younger brother, Harris Bigg-Wither. Harris was to inherit their father's riches, which included the estate of relatives named Wither. He could afford to marry whomever he chose, and on December 2, 1802, he proposed to Jane Austen. The match offered real advantages to a woman who, at nearly twenty-seven, was beyond the prime years for marriage. As Harris's wife, Jane never would have to worry about money. When he inherited his father's estate, Manydown would be their home, and she could invite Cassandra to live there, too. She would have a big, healthy, young husband—Harris was twenty-one. And most likely she would have children. So when Harris Bigg-Wither asked if she would marry him, Jane Austen said yes.

That night, laughter and rejoicing echoed through the stately halls of Manydown. But the next morning, Jane asked to see Harris alone. She had made a mistake and was calling off the engagement, she said. A marriage between Jane and Harris would have been a social contract and nothing more. They were old friends, but neither one loved the other. Although some women might marry first and wait for affection to grow, Jane's heart prevented her from marrying without love. Harris understood, but Jane and Cassandra could not consider staying on at Manydown. They left immediately for Steventon and returned to Bath the next day.

Fortunately for everyone concerned, no lasting harm was done. Harris Bigg-Wither bore the loss well. He married two years later and went on to father ten children and live the life of a respected country gentleman. The sisters Austen and Bigg remained friends, but Jane Austen received no more proposals of marriage.

As she traveled to all these places—to Dawlish, Lyme, Godmersham, Manydown, and Steventon—Jane toted the manuscripts of her three finished novels along with the rest of her luggage. She valued them too much to let them out of her sight.

But she wrote very little while she lived in Bath, for reasons that are unknown.

She kept alive her hope of being a published author, though, and her brother Henry helped her. Working through a lawyer friend, he offered her novel *Susan* to the London publisher Richard Crosby and Son in 1803. Crosby bought the manuscript for ten pounds and promised to publish it soon, but ignored it from then on.

While she waited to see *Susan* in print, Jane Austen began a new novel, titled *The Watsons*. This story centers on Emma Watson, the youngest of six grown children. Their father is a gentleman with no fortune, a widower and an invalid. Raised by an aunt who has recently married, Emma returns to live in her father's house. In just a few pages, Austen introduces Emma's quarrelsome family and transports her heroine to a ball. There, Emma catches the eye of the wealthy Lord Osborne and a local clergyman, Mr. Howard. She also meets the engaging Tom Musgrave, whom at least one of her sisters hopes to catch.

It appears that Austen planned to explore the pros and cons of marrying for money. "Poverty is a great Evil, but to a woman of Education & feeling it ought not, it cannot be the greatest," Emma tells her sister Elizabeth. Elizabeth responds, "I think I could like any good humoured Man with a comfortable Income." Austen made a promising start, but she never finished *The Watsons*. Modern readers can only guess why. Perhaps Emma Watson was too perfect a heroine, a young woman with no life lessons to learn.

Or did grief halt Jane Austen's progress? On December 16, 1804, her twenty-ninth birthday, her brother James encountered Anne Lefroy, the family friend who had encouraged Jane's writing but interfered in her love life. Mrs. Lefroy was out for a day of shopping in nearby Overton, accompanied by a servant. Like many gentlewomen, she enjoyed riding on horseback, but on this day she complained to James about her horse, calling it stupid and lazy. Then as she rode home, the horse bolted. The servant chased after his mistress but failed to catch the panicked steed. Mrs. Lefroy hung on, and when she thought it was safe, she tried to dismount. This was a mistake. She fell hard and died of her injuries a few hours later.

In future years, the coming of her birthday would remind Jane Austen of Anne Lefroy. On the day she turned thirty-three, December 16, 1808, Austen wrote a poem in tribute to her old neighbor. Mrs. Lefroy might have meddled, but Austen claimed to admire this "Angelic Woman." In her verses, she conjured up Mrs. Lefroy "as she used to be":

Her looks of eager Love, her accents sweet.
That voice & Countenance almost divine . . .
She speaks; 'tis Eloquence—that grace of Tongue
So rare, so lovely!—Never misapplied . . .
She speaks & reasons but on Virtue's side.

The first snows had barely fallen on Anne Lefroy's grave when the Reverend Austen fell ill. According to Jane, he suf-

The man in this illustration from a European medical text has had glass cups applied to his temples. A similar treatment failed to help Austen's father in his final illness.

fered from "oppression in the head with fever, violent tremulousness, & the greatest degree of Feebleness." His family sent for a doctor, who applied a remedy called cupping. The doctor placed heated glass cups on the patient's skin to draw blood toward the surface. But (no surprise) this treatment did nothing. The old man grew worse, and on January 21, 1805, he died. Jane sent a letter to her brother Frank, who was stationed aboard a ship off the English coast, informing him of the news. "Being quite insensible of his own state," she wrote, their father "was spared all the pain of separation, & he went off almost in his Sleep." She added these comforting words: "the Serenity of the Corpse is most delightful!"

five

AN EXTRAORDINARY FATE

Let other pens dwell on guilt and misery.
I quit such odious subjects as soon as I can.

—Mansfield Park

Seven years I suppose are enough to change every pore of one's skin, & every feeling of one's mind," observed Jane Austen in 1805. In 1798, she had been writing novels and dreaming of seeing them published. She could expect that when she left Steventon, it would be to live in her husband's home. Seven years later, she had put aside her writing like some childish thing. And her chances of marriage had faded with each passing year.

The Reverend Austen's death created a financial catastrophe for the surviving single women. The church had stopped paying his annuity when he died, leaving the women to depend on sons and brothers for support. James and Henry each gave them fifty pounds a year, but James, established in the parsonage at Steventon, might have given more. They expected another hundred from Edward, who could have easily shouldered all their expenses. Frank offered a hundred more, but his mother took only half, because he was engaged to be married and needed the money himself. If the women hoped for help from the wealthy Leigh-Perrots, Mrs. Austen's brother and his wife, they were disappointed again.

Jane and her mother and sister moved several times, always to cheaper lodgings, but even the rent for a small, shoddy flat in Bath was more than they could afford. Then kind Frank invited them to live in Southampton with him and his bride, Mary, after they married in 1806. His navy career took Frank away from home for long stretches, and he hated to leave Mary alone. The three Austen women agreed to the plan, because they really had no choice. Martha Lloyd, whose mother had recently died, was to join the household as well. Jane had never liked Bath, and after she left in July 1806, she never went back.

In Southampton the Austens lived in Castle Square. Their landlord, the Marquis of Landsdowne, dwelled with his wife in the neighboring gothic-style castle. The marquis's marriage had caused a local scandal, because his wife had been his mistress first. The Austens' house was old and needed repairs, but it had its charms. Its garden ran all the way to the old wall surrounding the town, and Jane looked forward to planting raspberries, gooseberries, currants, and roses. Living in

The castle built by the Austens' landlord and neighbor, the Marquis of Landsdowne, dominated the local landscape. Both the castle and the Austens' Southampton home have been torn down.

Southampton brought the women closer to Steventon, so they saw more of James, his Mary, and their children, including the new baby, Caroline. They also saw Edward and his family, who had begun spending time at Chawton House, a nearby estate that Edward had inherited. Jane went on shopping trips with Edward's oldest daughter, Fanny Knight, and enjoyed family outings.

Benefits can also be drawbacks, however, and her relatives got on Jane's nerves. She grew to dread visits from James. "His Chat seems all forced, his Opinions on many points too much copied from his Wife's," she grumbled, "& his time here is spent I think in walking about the House & banging the

Doors, or ringing the bell for a glass of water." Other family members made demands, too. Frank went to sea in early 1807, leaving the household of women to look after his pregnant wife. A daughter, Mary Jane, was born in April. (Frank's wife, Mary, would die in 1823 while giving birth to her eleventh child, a boy named Cholmeley, who lived only briefly.)

Jane had fun living with Martha Lloyd, though. They saw plays together and went to a ball where a dark-eyed gentleman surprised Jane by asking her to dance. Jane joked with her friend, pretending to believe that Martha was carrying on a forbidden love affair with a married clergyman.

She also escaped by making visits. She spent time with the Fowles—the Austens' old friends—and with the Biggs at Manydown. She never tired of seeing Henry and Eliza in London and going with them to concerts and dinner parties. Yet, as a poor woman, she traveled only when a male relative was going her way. Once she went to Godmersham, planning to stay two weeks, but her ride home fell through, and no one else was headed for Southampton. The hundred-mile trip required more than two days of travel, so her family decided that she should stay at Godmersham two more months, until Henry stopped there on his way to Hampshire.

Two months! This meant that Jane would miss a visit from the Bigg sisters—their last visit before Catherine Bigg was to be married. She appealed to Edward, but he refused to go out of his way so that she could see her women friends. So Jane lied and said she had a private reason for needing to be home, and

Edward had no choice. He took his sister to Southampton, but he made it clear that he was an important man, and she was wasting his time. "Till I have a travelling purse of my own, I must submit to such things," Jane lamented.

Yet Edward's sisters helped him selflessly. In September 1808, Cassandra went to Godmersham to aid Elizabeth with the birth of her eleventh child. Elizabeth delivered a healthy boy, Brook John, and seemed to be recovering. Then, without warning, she died, and her doctor had no idea why. Henry rushed to Godmersham, but Jane had to stay in Southampton and could only write letters to the family in Kent. She praised Elizabeth's "solid principles, her true devotion, her excellence in every relation of Life." She sympathized with "dearest Edward, whose loss & whose suffering seem to make those of every other person nothing." And she could not resist asking Cassandra, "I suppose you see the Corpse,—how does it appear?"

As the motherless family struggled to adjust, two of Edward's sons spent a few days in Southampton with their aunt Jane. She treated the boys with patient kindness and eased them through this sorrowful time. She took them to see a battleship being built and for a rowboat ride. She organized arts and crafts projects and games of cards and spillikins (pick-up sticks). "Her charm to children was great sweetness of manner—she seemed to love you, and you loved her naturally in return," remembered James's daughter Caroline. "She would tell us the most delightful stories chiefly of Fairyland, and her

Fairies had all characters of their own." Jane also joined in the children's games. "She would furnish us with what we wanted from her wardrobe, and she would often be the entertaining visitor in our make-believe house," Caroline said. Prim Cassandra preferred serious pastimes. She once lectured the children on astronomy, giving Fanny Knight a headache.

Even with Jane and Cassandra willing to care for their nephews and nieces, Frank and Mary were ready for a home of their own. They looked for one on the Isle of Wight, leaving Jane, Cassandra, their mother, and Martha Lloyd to worry again about where to live—but not for long. Edward offered them the choice of two houses that he owned. One was near Godmersham, in Kent, and the other was in Hampshire, close to his other estate, Chawton House. Mrs. Austen liked the place in Kent, but the others voted for Chawton Cottage. Edward remodeled it for the women, and they moved there in July 1809.

This "cottage" was a solid, two-story brick structure with six bedrooms and two parlors. One of the parlors held a piano. Mrs. Austen, who was seventy, took charge of the garden. She was often outside in her green apron, digging up potatoes or caring for the flowers, vegetables, and fruit trees. The house sat close to the busy, noisy Winchester Road, so from time to time she left her work to watch the passing traffic.

"The awful stillness of night" would be "frequently broken by the sound of passing carriages, which seemed sometimes even to shake the bed," said Caroline Austen, who liked to stay with her grandmother and aunts. Caroline observed that her

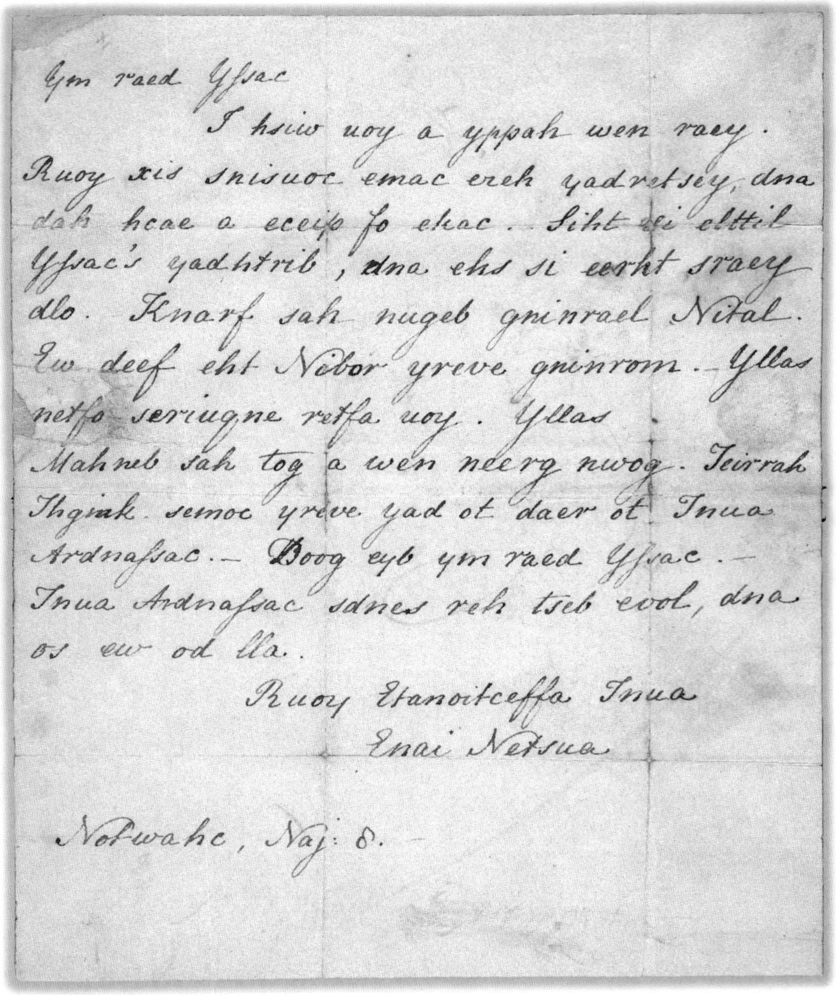
Ym raed Yssac
I hsiw uoy a yppah wen raey.
Ruoy xis snisuoc emac ereh yadretsey, dna
dah hcae a eceip fo ekac. Siht si elttil
Yssac's yadhtrib, dna ehs si eerht sraey
dlo. Knarf sah nugeb gninrael Nital.
Ew deef eht Nibor yreve gninrom. Yllas
netfo seriuqne retfa uoy. Yllas
Mahneb sah tog a wen neerg nwog. Teirrah
Thgink semoc yreve yad ot daer ot Tnua
Ardnassac. Doog eyb ym raed Yssac.
Tnua Ardnassac sdnes reh tseb evol, dna
os ew od lla.
Ruoy Etanoitceffa Tnua
Enai Netsua

Notwahc, Naj: 8.

A favorite aunt of the children in her family, Jane Austen wrote this letter to her niece Cassy, Charles's oldest girl, reversing the spelling of all the words.

aunt Jane wore a white cloth cap indoors. "Such was the custom with the ladies who were not quite young," she noted. "My two Aunts were not accounted very good dressers, and were thought to have taken to the garb of middle age unnecessarily soon." Caroline's brother, James Edward, remembered that Aunt Jane's neighbors "often served for her amusement." She "was as far as possible from being censorious or satirical," he explained. "The laugh which she occasionally raised was by imagining for her neighbors, as she was equally ready to imagine for her friends or herself, impossible contingencies . . . or in writing a fictitious history of what they were supposed to have said or done."

Jane rose early in Chawton. She practiced the piano before the others were awake, and then she prepared everyone's breakfast. In Chawton, she felt settled for the first time since leaving Steventon, and at last she found the hours and the space to write in earnest. She worked at a small desk in the parlor that held the piano. She kept her writing secret from the servants and neighbors and hurriedly hid her manuscript pages when someone entered the room.

Remembering her novel *Susan,* she wrote to Richard Crosby, the publisher who had paid ten pounds for it in 1803 and never printed it. Using a name that she invented, "Mrs. Ashton Dennis," she claimed to be the author of this work. Six years had passed, so she assumed that Crosby had lost the manuscript, and she offered to supply a new one. Crosby replied that he still had the book, but he was in no hurry to publish it. Mrs. Dennis could have it back if she repaid his ten pounds.

Ten pounds! This was more than a poor spinster could afford. So she dusted off *Sense and Sensibility,* the novel featuring the sisters Elinor and Marianne, and sent it to a different publisher, Thomas Egerton. Unwilling to take a financial risk on an unknown female writer, Egerton offered to publish this novel if the author paid the costs. Again Austen faced the same old obstacle: money. But this time Henry and Eliza came to her rescue and paid for the book to be printed.

Printing a book took a long time in Jane Austen's day, when type was set by hand, letter by letter. In March 1811, Jane stayed with Henry and Eliza in London while she looked over the proofs—the first, unbound printed pages of her book. Then

Printing was a slow, tedious task in the 1800s. Three workers operate an English printing press by hand.

she waited eagerly for the finished book to appear. "I can no more forget it, than a mother can forget her sucking child," she said. At last, in October, *Sense and Sensibility* was published anonymously, in three volumes.

The novel focuses on sisters Elinor and Marianne Dashwood, who are forced out of their home after their father's death. Elinor possesses "strength of understanding and coolness of judgment"; she displays good sense by keeping her emotions in check. Marianne, meanwhile, indulges in sensibility, or feeling. She is "eager in every thing," Austen wrote; "her sorrows, her joys, could have no moderation." The person forcing the women out is their weak-willed half brother, John. The son of their father's first wife, he has inherited the family estate. Although he promised his father to take care of Elinor, Marianne, and their mother and younger sister, he lets his greedy wife, Fanny, talk him out of doing what is right.

Mrs. Dashwood's wealthy cousin, Sir John Middleton, offers the women a home at Barton Cottage, where they will be his neighbors. Sir John hates to be alone and surrounds himself with company. He is constantly dropping by to invite the women to dinner parties. He introduces them to his friend Colonel Brandon, but Marianne dismisses the colonel as "an absolute old bachelor, for he was on the wrong side of five and thirty." Surely a man of his great age was too old to be in love! "He talked of flannel waistcoats," Marianne says, and she connects these practical garments "with aches, cramps, rheumatisms, and every species of ailment that can afflict the old and the feeble." She

Carried her down the hill.

Willoughby rescues Marianne in an illustration from an early edition of *Sense and Sensibility.*

prefers the younger Mr. Willoughby, who rescued her when she turned her ankle while walking in the countryside.

Marianne spends so much time with Willoughby and the pair is so intimate that Elinor wonders if they are secretly engaged. While Marianne's behavior invites speculation, Elinor's hides her most cherished feelings: she secretly loves Edward Ferrars, the brother of her sister-in-law, Fanny Dashwood, and hopes he cares for her in return.

Lady Middleton's sister, Charlotte Palmer, pays a visit and turns out to be the empty-headed product of a girls' school. Her husband cannot bear her foolishness. He buries himself in a newspaper and looks up only to make rude remarks. Elinor thinks that Mr. Palmer was captivated by his wife's beauty and discovered too late that "he was the husband of a very silly woman." Two wheedling sisters, Nancy and Lucy Steele, visit as well. They fawn over the Middletons' spoiled children to gain the parents' favor. Greed, stupidity, bad manners, ambition: Austen portrayed a harsh society that is quick to pass judgment.

Conniving Lucy Steele tells Elinor that she is secretly engaged to Edward Ferrars, and this news cuts Elinor to the heart. She suffers inwardly, but "though her complexion varied, she stood firm . . . and felt in no danger of an hysterical fit, or a swoon."

The action moves to London, where Marianne hopes to see Willoughby again. The longed-for meeting takes place at a party, where Willoughby tries his best to ignore Marianne.

When this becomes impossible, he addresses her formally, and he escapes as fast as he can. Soon afterward, Marianne learns the reason for his coldness: Willoughby is engaged to someone else, a young woman with money. Marianne, predictably, collapses in grief. Yet Colonel Brandon then tells Elinor that things have turned out for the best, because Willoughby is a scoundrel, the man who seduced a young woman under his guardianship.

While in London, Nancy Steele reveals the secret of her sister's engagement. Instead of being happy for her son, Edward Ferrars's overbearing mother disapproves of the match and is

An unhappily married couple like Mr. and Mrs. Palmer was a source of humor for artists and writers in many periods of history, including Austen's.

Emma Thompson played sensible Elinor Dashwood, and Kate Winslet was the more emotional Marianne, in the 1995 film *Sense and Sensibility.*

furious. She disinherits Edward and makes her younger son, Robert, her heir. The engagement was a youthful mistake on Edward's part, but Lucy refuses to release him from his promise, and he is duty-bound to honor it.

On their way home to Barton, the sisters stop at the country home of addle-brained Charlotte Palmer and her rude husband. There, Marianne walks outdoors in bad weather, carelessly risking her health, and falls gravely ill. Colonel Brandon shows his fine character by traveling to Barton to fetch Mrs. Dashwood, but before they return, Willoughby shows up. He tells Elinor a long story of his past errors: how lavish spending and a small income landed him in debt; how he behaved wrongly toward

Colonel Brandon's ward yet believed she was not free of blame; how he meant only to toy with Marianne's affection but fell in love with her. He admits to Elinor that although he is married to someone else, he still loves Marianne.

Jane Austen's handwritten versions of *Sense and Sensibility* were lost, so they cannot be compared to the printed book. It is impossible to know how she shaped her work over time. Willoughby's lengthy speech sounds artificial—more like something written than spoken. It reminds readers that Austen first wrote this novel as a series of letters. Most likely everything Willoughby says was written in a letter in an earlier version.

The plot resolves neatly for both sisters. Marianne is recovering when her mother arrives. Being ill has given her time to think. Having learned to rein in her emotions, she sees the worth of Colonel Brandon, who has loved her all along, and agrees to be his wife. Marianne "was born to discover the falsehood of her own opinions, and to counteract, by her own conduct, her most favourite maxims," Austen concludes. "She was born to overcome an affection formed so late in life as at seventeen, and . . . voluntarily to give her hand to another!" The other was a man "she had considered too old to be married,—and who still sought the constitutional safeguard of a flannel waistcoat!" Marianne has grown up.

Elinor is resigned to disappointment when she learns that "Mr. Ferrars is married," but she soon gets a happy surprise. Lucy Steele has schemed to marry Robert Ferrars, the younger brother, who is in line to inherit his mother's fortune. Edward, freed from his obligation to Lucy, proposes marriage to Elinor. Old Mrs. Ferrars feels a morsel of tenderness toward her older son and gives him some money—just enough to wed. Married to men of good character, the sisters live out their lives in contentment.

Even Willoughby lives happily ever after. He recalls Marianne with regret, but Austen cautions her readers against thinking that "he fled from society, or contracted an habitual gloom of temper, or died of a broken heart." Willoughby, she states, "lived to exert, and frequently to enjoy himself."

Sense and Sensibility received two good reviews in the press. One book critic praised the author's "intimate knowledge of life." He recommended the novel to "female friends," because it might teach them "many sober and salutary maxims for the conduct of life." The other critic noted that the book "is well written; the characters are in genteel life, naturally drawn, and judiciously supported. The incidents are probable, and highly pleasing, and interesting; the conclusion such as the reader must wish it should be. . . ."

The Countess of Bessborough, a member of stylish society, disagreed on the last point. "It is a clever Novel," she commented. "And tho' it ends stupidly I was much amus'd by it." The countess never described the ending she would have liked better.

Austen's book found at least one fan in the royal family. "'Sence and Sencibility' I have *just finished* reading; it certainly is interesting, & you feel quite one of the company," wrote sixteen-year-old Princess Charlotte to her close friend, Miss Mercer Elphinstone. "Maryanne & me are very like in *disposition*." The princess's careless spelling tried the patience of her grandfather, King George III, who had sat on the throne while Britain lost the American Revolution. The king had gradually been slipping into insanity, and in January 1811, Charlotte's father, the future King George IV, began ruling in his place as the Prince Regent.

Concluding her first published book, Austen wrote that "Marianne Dashwood was born to an extraordinary fate." But

The public adored Princess Charlotte. When she died in childbirth at age twenty-one, all of England mourned. "From the highest to the lowest, this death was felt as a calamity that demanded the intense sorrow of domestic misfortune," recalled the writer Harriet Martineau.

was Austen's own fate any less remarkable? Thomas Egerton had sold every copy of *Sense and Sensibility* by summer 1813, and Austen had earned 140 pounds. For the first time, she had money to spend. The novel's success so delighted Egerton that he offered to print another book by the same author—and this time it would cost her nothing. In fact, he paid her 110 pounds for *First Impressions*. Another book with this title had come out in 1801, so Austen's book was published in January 1813 as *Pride and Prejudice*.

six

LIGHT, BRIGHT, AND SPARKLING

Pride relates more to our opinion of ourselves; vanity, to what we would have others think of us.

—Pride and Prejudice

PRIDE AND *PREJUDICE* opens with one of the most famous sentences ever written: "It is a truth universally acknowledged, that a single man in possession of a good fortune, must be in want of a wife." With these words, Jane Austen announced to her readers that they were about to meet such a man and the people eager to marry him off. What was more, they were going to have fun. The dark cynicism of *Sense and Sensibility* was largely gone, blown away by a clean, fresh wind.

The action begins when the young man, Mr. Bingley, rents a country house called Netherfield. His coming is good news for his neighbor Mrs. Bennet, whose husband has a small income. She has five daughters, and finding them husbands is "the business of her life."

The Bennets encounter Mr. Bingley at a local ball, which he attends with his sisters and his friend, Fitzwilliam Darcy. Each young man makes a strong impression. Bingley pleases with his looks and manners, and he endears himself to Mrs. Bennet by dancing with her oldest daughter, Jane. Bingley and Jane quickly fall in love. But, like Elinor Dashwood, Jane is expert at hiding her feelings.

Aloof Mr. Darcy, handsomer and even richer than his friend, gets off to a bad start by declining to ask Elizabeth Bennet to dance. He sums her up as "tolerable; but not handsome enough to tempt *me.*" Elizabeth overhears this remark and instantly dislikes proud Mr. Darcy, later amusing her friends with the story of Darcy's snub. She cannot know that Darcy spoke too quickly. No sooner did he pass judgment on her looks than he began to find her face "rendered uncommonly intelligent by the beautiful expression of her dark eyes."

Lizzy Bennet is easily the most captivating character in all Jane Austen's books. She is outspoken, witty, and smart enough to learn from experience. "Elizabeth has a thousand faults," noted a critic in 1898. She "is often blind, pert, audacious, imprudent; and yet how splendidly she comes out of it all! Alive to the very tips of her fingers." Like Austen, Elizabeth studies human nature. "People themselves alter so much, that there is something new to be observed in them for ever," she says. Her creator felt fond of Elizabeth, too. "I must confess that *I* think

"She is tolerable": Darcy looks down on Elizabeth Bennet in this illustration from an 1894 edition of *Pride and Prejudice.*

her as delightful a creature as ever appeared in print," Austen admitted. "How I shall be able to tolerate those who do not like *her* at least, I do not know."

By the novel's end, Elizabeth will have taught Darcy to quell his pride, and she will have overcome her wrong first impression. She and Darcy both will discover that ill will can mask attraction. They will learn to understand the contents of their hearts, but this kind of learning takes time.

Elizabeth, like many young people, is embarrassed by her

family. She has good reason to be uneasy. Her younger sisters talk of nothing but soldiers and balls; her mother speaks and acts without thinking. Even her father lacks social graces. A man with a dry wit, Mr. Bennet amuses himself by making fun of his wife and daughters. He hides in his library rather than offer his family guidance.

When soldiers are quartered in a nearby town, Elizabeth feels drawn to one of them, the dashing but penniless Wickham. Mr. Wickham is quick to confirm her first impression of

People like the Bennets and Bingleys entertained one another by making music, although some performed better than others. Here two girls show off their musical accomplishments to guests who are less impressed than their parents.

Darcy, whom he has known since boyhood. He tells her that Darcy's father was his godfather. The older Mr. Darcy had promised to make Wickham the pastor of a church on his estate, but after the old man died, young Darcy spitefully gave the living to someone else. Darcy resented his father's love for his godson, Wickham says. Still smarting, perhaps, from Darcy's insult, Elizabeth is all too ready to believe the charming Wickham.

Another young man turns up as well. This one is a humorous buffoon who lacks brains but is full of self-importance. After all, he is the clergyman on the estate of rich, pompous Lady Catherine de Bourgh—who happens to be Mr. Darcy's aunt. This guest, Mr. Collins, is a cousin of Elizabeth's father. Because of the laws that governed inheritance, he stands to take possession of the Bennets' home when Mr. Bennet dies. Lady Catherine has decided that Mr. Collins should marry, so he visits the Bennets to find a wife. Almost immediately, he proposes to Elizabeth.

She turns him down, and no matter what she says, he refuses to believe that her no means *no*. "It is usual with young ladies to reject the addresses of the man whom they secretly mean to accept, when he first applies for their favour," Mr. Collins declares. Elizabeth repeats her refusal but cannot make herself understood. At last, in frustration, she asks, "Can I speak plainer?" But Collins merely calls her charming.

Collins is stunned and briefly insulted when he finally understands that Elizabeth has rejected him. Soon it is Elizabeth's turn to be shocked, though, because Collins promptly asks her friend Charlotte Lucas to marry him. Charlotte is twenty-seven and possesses neither money nor beauty, so when Collins offers her a chance to have a home and family, she grabs it. The wrong choice for Elizabeth is the right one for Charlotte.

At this point, things start to go wrong. Not only does Wickham transfer his attention to a girl with a large inheritance, but Bingley suddenly leaves for London. Elizabeth suspects that his sisters and Darcy want to keep him away from Jane.

Elizabeth visits her newly married friend, Charlotte, and meets the high-and-mighty Lady Catherine, who likes minding other people's business. Elizabeth also bumps into Mr. Darcy, who is staying with his aunt. Before long, Darcy gives Elizabeth the surprise of her life when he confesses that he loves her. He proposes marriage, although his judgment reminds him that she is inferior. She rejects the offer and angrily accuses Darcy of hurting Jane by spoiling her chances with Bingley, and of doing wrong to Wickham.

In the world of Jane Austen's novels, characters write letters to relate what they cannot say in person. Darcy writes a letter—a very long one—to Elizabeth, hoping to explain himself. He admits that he separated Bingley from Jane, but he had watched Jane and concluded that she had formed a weak attachment to his friend. He hoped to save Bingley from "a most unhappy connection." He objected to "the total want of propriety" displayed by Elizabeth's mother, her younger sisters, and, at times, her father.

In 1940's *Pride and Prejudice,* Lady Catherine de Bourgh (actor Edna May Oliver) gives unwanted advice to Elizabeth Bennet (played by Greer Garson).

Darcy also sets the record straight about Wickham. Elizabeth learns that Wickham is a good-for-nothing on a par with Willoughby in *Sense and Sensibility.* He had tried to seduce Darcy's sister, Georgiana, and rightly earned the family's scorn.

Darcy's letter makes Elizabeth furious—at first. Then it makes her think, and she reads it again after she has calmed down. This time, she concludes that what Darcy wrote about Wickham must be true, and her opinion of Darcy starts to change. He seems proud, but Bingley, who knows him well, holds him in high regard. How could Bingley be wrong? Elizabeth feels shame at the way Darcy described her family, but she admits that his words are just.

Her first impression of Darcy was wrong, and Elizabeth is ashamed of herself for speaking ill of him. "How despicably I have acted!" she cries out. "I, who have valued myself on my abilities!" This is a key point in the novel. It is painful for Elizabeth to see her own faults, but she is wiser for doing so. "Till this moment, I never knew myself," she says, and she is right.

Elizabeth welcomes the chance to travel in the country with her aunt and uncle, Mr. and Mrs. Gardiner. English people on holiday commonly toured fine country houses, and Mrs. Gardiner wants to see Darcy's estate, Pemberley. Elizabeth agrees to go along only when she learns that Darcy is away from home. But seeing the miles of beautiful woodland that surround the great house and the lofty, elegant rooms within causes her regret. Elizabeth thinks that "to be mistress of Pemberley might be something!" She and the Gardiners bump into the master of Pemberley unexpectedly when he returns a day early. He is a changed man, a different Darcy, one who generously offers them hospitality.

Then, suddenly, a catastrophe befalls the Bennet family. The no-good Wickham has run up huge debts and taken off with Lydia Bennet, a sister of Jane and Elizabeth. This couple must be found. To have a sister living with a man, unmarried, will ruin the reputations of all the Bennet girls and destroy their chances of marrying well. Luckily for everyone, Mr. Gar-

Austen's visits to great homes like Edward's Hampshire estate, Chawton House, helped her describe Pemberley.

diner tracks down the couple in London, persuades Wickham to marry Lydia, and settles his debts—or so the Bennets believe. Flighty Mrs. Bennet is thrilled to have a married daughter, regardless of how the match came about.

When Lydia comes home in triumph with her husband, she lets it slip to Elizabeth that Darcy attended her wedding. Elizabeth appeals to her aunt for information, but Mrs. Gardiner expresses surprise. Didn't Elizabeth know that it was really Darcy who found the runaway couple, paid off Wickham, and arranged the wedding? Weren't Elizabeth and Darcy soon to be engaged?

If only they were! Elizabeth now knows that if Darcy

proposed again, she would gratefully accept. "She began now to comprehend that he was exactly the man, who, in disposition and talents, would most suit her," Austen wrote. Sadly, marriage to Darcy is now out of the question, Elizabeth believes.

More surprising things happen, though. Bingley returns to Netherfield, promptly calls on the Bennets, and proposes to Jane. Next, arrogant Lady Catherine turns up and demands to speak privately with Elizabeth. She insists, strangely, that Elizabeth must never marry Darcy, whom she intends to be the husband of her daughter. Her plan is not to be thwarted by "the upstart pretensions of a young woman without family, connections, or fortune." Elizabeth defends her right to marry Darcy, even though she has no hope that such a marriage will take place: "He is a gentleman; I am a gentleman's daughter; so far we are equal." "True. You *are* a gentleman's daughter," the great lady replies. "But who was your mother? Who are your uncles and aunts?" An enraged Lady Catherine leaves in a huff, having shown herself to be cruder than the lower-born Mrs. Bennet.

Darcy learns of Elizabeth's spirited reply to his aunt, and it gives him hope. When he next meets Elizabeth and she thanks him for helping her family, he replies that he thought only of her happiness. "*My* affections and wishes are unchanged," he confesses.

Throughout most of *Pride and Prejudice,* Jane Austen closely followed Elizabeth's thoughts and related everything that she and Darcy said to each other. But at this crucial moment, she did something curious; she chose to be brief. Elizabeth, she wrote,

> *gave him to understand that her sentiments had undergone so material a change, since the period to which he alluded, as to make her receive with gratitude and pleasure, his present assurances. The happiness which this reply produced, was such as he had probably never felt before; and he expressed himself on this occasion as sensibly and as warmly as a man violently in love can be supposed to do.*

Some readers have felt cheated by this description. They looked forward to a great love scene, and Austen gave them a summary. They have accused the author of losing interest in her story once the characters solve their problems, and rushing its conclusion. A few critics have even said that a spinster like Jane Austen would have had no inkling what people in love might say at a time like this, so she could not possibly have written it.

Maybe Austen knew what she was doing, though. By describing the meeting between Elizabeth and Darcy in this way, she stressed the universal nature of their experience. She wrote about two young people in England in the late 1700s, but they are the same as lovers in any place and time. This is why readers everywhere can hear in their minds the words Elizabeth uses to receive Darcy's assurance of his love. They know exactly how sensibly and warmly a man in love behaves.

Elizabeth accepts Darcy this time, of course. She puts up with the comments of her astonished family, who thought he was the last man she would ever choose. "We all know him to be a proud, unpleasant sort of man," Mr. Bennet tells Elizabeth, speaking of Darcy; "but this would be nothing if you really liked him."

Pride and Prejudice, "By the Author of *Sense and Sensibility,*" was an instant hit. One reviewer called it "very far superior to almost all the publications of the kind which have lately come before us." Another critic praised Austen's characters, insisting that every member of the Bennet family "excites the interest." Still, Elizabeth stood out, because her "sense and conduct are of a superior order to those of the common heroines of novels."

"The work is rather too light & bright & sparkling," Jane Austen wrote, pretending to find fault with her novel. "It wants to be stretched out here & there with a long Chapter," she continued, "about something unconnected with the story; an Essay on Writing, a critique on Walter Scott, or the history of Buonaparte." After a long, boring digression, the reader would return "with increased delight to the playfulness . . . of the general stile."

The Austens all liked *Pride and Prejudice.* Jane read the book aloud to her niece Fanny Knight, who was often at Chawton. "[Aunt Jane] & I had a delicious morning together," Fanny noted in her diary. Charles Austen reported that some of his fellow naval officers had read and enjoyed it. Jane tried to confine knowledge of her authorship to her family and close friends, but word was getting out. "The Secret has spread so far as to be scarcely the Shadow of a secret now," she wrote to Frank Austen. Their brother Henry had the toughest time keeping mum. More than once, Jane continued, Henry has heard people praise *Pride and Prejudice,* "& what does he do in the warmth of his Brotherly vanity & Love, but immediately tell them who wrote it!" Jane tried to harden herself to the fact that her name was becoming known.

A great book brings forth strong opinions, and Austen's second published novel has had its detractors. Mary Russell Mitford, a novelist and playwright of Austen's day, thought Elizabeth Bennet was too smart-alecky to appeal to a man like Darcy. "Wickham is equally bad," she wrote. "Oh! They were just fit for each other, and I cannot forgive that delightful Darcy for parting them." Not only *Pride and Prejudice,* but all Jane Austen's books annoyed a writer from a later era, the popular American author and humorist Mark Twain. "Every time I read *Pride and Prejudice,* I want to dig her up and hit her over the skull with her own shin-bone," he ranted. Twain acknowledged that Austen's novels have value, but "the thing involved is purely a matter of *taste,*" he wrote. Everyone finds "that there are fine things, great things, admirable things, which others can perceive and they can't," he noted. For him, Jane Austen's genius fell into this category.

That spring, Jane broke away from enjoyment of her literary success to go to London, escorted by Edward's oldest son.

Henry had summoned her to nurse his wife, her much-loved cousin and sister-in-law, Eliza, through the final days of a fatal illness. Eliza is thought to have had breast cancer, the disease that killed her mother. Eliza died on April 25, 1813, at age fifty, and was buried beside her son and mother. Her epitaph, composed by the grieving Henry, praised her as "a woman of brilliant generous and cultivated mind," one who was just and charitable. Her death was "much regretted by the wise and good and deeply lamented by the poor."

This commercial section of London bustled with life in 1805. By 1800, London was a city of a million people and a center of trade, finance, and diplomacy. "London possesses those grand features which characterized ancient Rome: it is the seat of liberty, the mart of intellect, and the envy of nations," noted a writer of the time.

Jane left her bereaved brother on May 1, but Henry brought her back to London before the month ended. Together they toured art exhibitions, and Jane had fun searching for her characters' portraits among the paintings she saw. She quickly spotted one that could have been Jane Bingley: "exactly herself, size, shaped face, features & sweetness. . . . She is dressed in a white gown, with green ornaments, which convinces me of what I had always supposed, that green was a favourite colour with her." She hunted in vain for Elizabeth Darcy's likeness. "I can only imagine that Mr. D. prizes any Picture of her too much to like it should be exposed to the public eye," she concluded. Then she went home again, and, despite a mysterious pain in her face, she spent two months completing *Mansfield Park,* her first novel written after leaving Steventon.

The years were outrunning the wind. Austen's oldest nieces, Anna Austen and Fanny Knight, turned twenty in 1813. Both reached out to their aunt Jane for advice. Jane counseled Anna, who was writing a novel, to be sure her characters' behavior was consistent with their nature. She explained, for example, that "Mrs. F. is not careful enough of Susan's health;—Susan ought not to be walking out so soon after Heavy rains, taking long walks in the dirt. An anxious Mother would not suffer it." She encouraged Anna to keep writing. "You are but *now* coming to the heart & beauty of your book; till the heroine grows up, the fun must be imperfect. . . . One does not care for girls till they are grown up."

Jane advised Fanny on matters of the heart. When Fanny

was expecting a marriage proposal from a modest, sensible young man of good character, Austen urged her "not to think of accepting him unless you really do like him. Anything is to be preferred or endured rather than marrying without Affection." Fanny heeded her aunt's advice. If the gentleman proposed, she turned him down.

Henry visited Chawton in the summer of 1813, and so did Charles, the baby of the family, who in 1807 had married his love, seventeen-year-old Frances Palmer. Frances was an English girl with no fortune who was raised in Bermuda. By 1813, Charles and Frances had three little daughters. A year later, Frances would become the next Austen bride to die of complications from childbirth.

seven

VICE AND VIRTUE

What strange creatures we are!

—letter to Fanny Knight, November 18, 1814

JANE AUSTEN'S characters courted and married between the covers of books, sheltered from the world outside. Yet here and there, Austen hinted that war and politics sometimes drew people's attention away from love. The army regiment that appears in *Pride and Prejudice* reminds readers that Britain and France were at war.

From the 1790s through 1815, the British were either fighting the French or expecting them to invade. Proclaiming it their duty to free other oppressed people of Europe, the French had expanded their control into the Netherlands, Italy, and several German states. Great Britain and other nations hoped to halt

France's conquest of its neighbors, because it threatened European stability. The warring intensified after 1799, when a power-hungry army officer named Napoleon Bonaparte seized control in France. In 1812, the British and their allies thwarted Napoleon in his attempt to invade Russia. A year later, they won a major conflict with his forces at Leipzig, in Germany. They finally defeated him in the Battle of Waterloo, fought in present-day Belgium, in June 1815.

As part of its wartime strategy, Britain tried to block U.S. ships from trading with France. The crews of British ships also seized sailors from American vessels and forced them into service for the Crown. These practices infuriated the Americans, and in 1812, the United States declared war on Great Britain. This conflict, known as the War of 1812, lasted three years and had no clear winner.

While their soldiers and sailors clashed with enemies on land and sea, the British royalty behaved shamefully. The Prince Regent was notoriously corrupt. He had married his cousin Caroline of Brunswick only because he had run up huge debts. He knew that Parliament would raise his allowance if he had a wife. The prince was in love with his mistress, hated his wife, and spent no more than one night with her—just long enough to father Princess Charlotte. Caroline was no better. She slept with a string of lovers before and after her marriage, and is thought to have had an illegitimate son. Still, when her husband declared her an unfit mother and decreed that the princess was not to see her, she had Jane Austen's

It's a Blessing to be Happy and Contented.
Well as this Purse must go to Knight
Ill make the most of it
Chamber

King George IV, the former Prince Regent, kisses his mistress in this political cartoon from 1822. Meanwhile, he ignores his government and family responsibilities.

sympathy. "Poor Woman, I shall support her as long as I can, because she *is* a Woman, & because I hate her Husband," Austen declared.

In 1811, the Duke of Clarence caused another stir. The duke, who was the prince's brother William and a future king of England, kicked his mistress and their ten children out of the home they shared and began chasing after rich young women. "Heaven defend any poor girl from marrying him," wrote Princess Charlotte to her friend Miss Elphinstone.

Such dreadful goings-on! Many Britons worried that the

upper classes were setting a bad example for the nation's youth. The heroine of Austen's next novel, *Mansfield Park,* meets some of these misguided young people.

Fanny Price is nine years old when she leaves her large, struggling family in Portsmouth and goes to live at Mansfield Park. The estate is home to her uncle and aunt, Sir Thomas and Lady Bertram, and their four children. The Bertrams treat Fanny well enough, but she is reminded often of her humble background. She is told by another aunt, the conniving, selfish Mrs. Norris, "Wherever you are, you must be the lowest and last."

Years pass, and Fanny grows into a virtuous teenager. Her cousin Tom, in contrast, is an extravagant youth who runs up debts. Tom's sisters, Maria and Julia, are proud and womanly, but their moral education has been neglected. Their mother cares chiefly about her needlework and her little dog, and their father is satisfied so long as they appear outwardly accomplished. Only Fanny's cousin Edmund, who plans to be a clergyman, resembles her in spirit. For Fanny, feelings of friendship for Edmund develop into love that she keeps secret from him and everyone else.

Into the neighborhood come two "young people of fortune." Henry and Mary Crawford are a brother and sister who have been exposed to the "vicious conduct"—the vices—prevailing in high society. Mary toys with the idea of falling in love with Tom Bertram, who is in line to inherit his father's estate. But when Tom sails to the West Indies with his father, she turns her attention to Edmund, causing Fanny much worry. Mary tries to persuade Edmund to give up the idea of a career in the church, and not only because it pays so little. Mary has been taught that clergymen are lazy and lacking in ambition. "Be honest and poor, by all means—but I shall not envy you," Mary says. "I have a much greater respect for those that are honest and rich." Mary's brother boldly flirts with both Bertram sisters, even though Maria is engaged to rich, empty-headed Mr. Rushworth. Breaking hearts feeds Henry Crawford's vanity.

Tom returns from overseas before his father and invites to Mansfield Park a friend, Mr. Yates. This gentleman has one thing on his mind: the theater. He suggests that they all stage a play, as the Austen brothers did at Steventon. The idea excites the young people—everyone but Fanny and Edmund. While the others learn lines and practice scenes, the pious pair fuss and fret. It seems the chosen play, *Lovers' Vows*, is all wrong for youthful actors. The title means nothing today, but readers in Jane Austen's time knew that *Lovers' Vows* dealt with sex outside of marriage and an illegitimate birth. Edmund finally gives in to Mary Crawford's pressure and takes a part, but Fanny remains firm. Soon, as Fanny feared, rehearsals lead to flirting and jealousy among the performers at Mansfield Park.

Sir Thomas comes home, putting an end to the theatrics, and Maria Bertram marries Mr. Rushworth. Fanny then enjoys a visit from her favorite brother, William, who has embarked on a naval career. "Children of the same family, the same blood, with the same first associations and habits, have some means of enjoyment in their power, which no subsequent connections can supply," wrote Austen. As someone from a large family, Austen knew this kind of enjoyment well. Happy in William's company, Fanny has no idea that she is about to face another test of character. Henry Crawford tells his sister that he has decided to make Fanny fall in love with him. "Fanny Price! Nonsense! No, no. You ought to be satisfied with her two cousins," Mary says. "But I cannot be satisfied without Fanny Price," Henry insists, "without making a small hole in Fanny Price's heart."

Henry Crawford may have outsmarted himself, though. As he pays special attention to Fanny—and she staunchly resists—he is the one who falls in love. Crawford proposes marriage, which horrifies Fanny but delights Sir Thomas, who sees a fine opportunity for his niece. The conflict between her duty to her uncle and her distaste for the values that Crawford represents is too much for Fanny to bear. She understands "how wretched, and how unpardonable" it is "to marry without affection," and she breaks down. Sir Thomas wisely sends her away, to visit her family in Portsmouth for the first time since coming to Mansfield Park.

Fanny has forgotten much about her early years in Portsmouth. Her family's house is smaller and dirtier than she remembers. Her father drinks, and her overworked mother lets the children run wild. Fanny misses Mansfield Park as the months pass, but the Bertrams make no effort to bring her back. Fanny, like Jane Austen for much of her life, is a single

Sir Thomas Bertram shows displeasure when Fanny Price declines Henry Crawford's proposal in the 1999 film *Mansfield Park*. Harold Pinter and Frances O'Connor portray Sir Thomas and Fanny.

woman without money whose ability to travel depends on the whims of others.

At least new surroundings can cause a person to learn and grow, and this is what happens to Fanny in Portsmouth. Amid the filth and confusion of her family's home, she examines her life from a fresh point of view. Her opinion of Henry Crawford, in particular, starts to change. Henry advances William's naval career by introducing him to his uncle, an admiral. Then he comes to Portsmouth to see Fanny and treats her family with respect. The story is getting interesting, because Fanny seems to be breaking free from the moral cage that has kept her from seeing that people are neither all good nor all bad. Will she learn to like Henry Crawford, and possibly to love him?

Not a chance. Letters reach Portsmouth, one after another, bringing all kinds of terrible news that can hardly be believed. First, Fanny learns that Tom Bertram is ill—so ill, in fact, that the family doubts he will recover. More than Tom's life is in the balance, because if he dies, Edmund becomes their father's heir. Having a fortune to inherit would make Edmund more attractive to Mary Crawford. Fanny next learns that after quitting Portsmouth, Henry Crawford chased after her cousin Maria; he has persuaded Maria to leave her husband and run off with him. Also, Julia has eloped with stage-struck Mr. Yates. But at last her aunt and uncle summon Fanny home.

The story ends happily for some characters and not so well for others. Tom Bertram recovers and mends his free-spending ways. Julia marries Yates. Crawford abandons Maria, who goes to live with her mean-spirited aunt, Mrs. Norris, having disgraced herself and her family. Mary Crawford, meanwhile, sees nothing more than "folly" in her brother's elopement with Maria. The only thing to regret, she says, is that the public learned of the affair. Edmund's eyes have been opened to Mary's moral shallowness and he sees that Fanny would be his ideal wife. Life goes on at Mansfield Park, with Fanny's sister Susan taking her place as the adopted niece.

Mansfield Park was published in May 1814. It is a somber book, lacking the spark of *Pride and Prejudice.* Although these books appeared within two years of each other, a long span of time separated their composition. *Pride and Prejudice* was a novel of Austen's hopeful youth; she wrote *Mansfield Park* as a

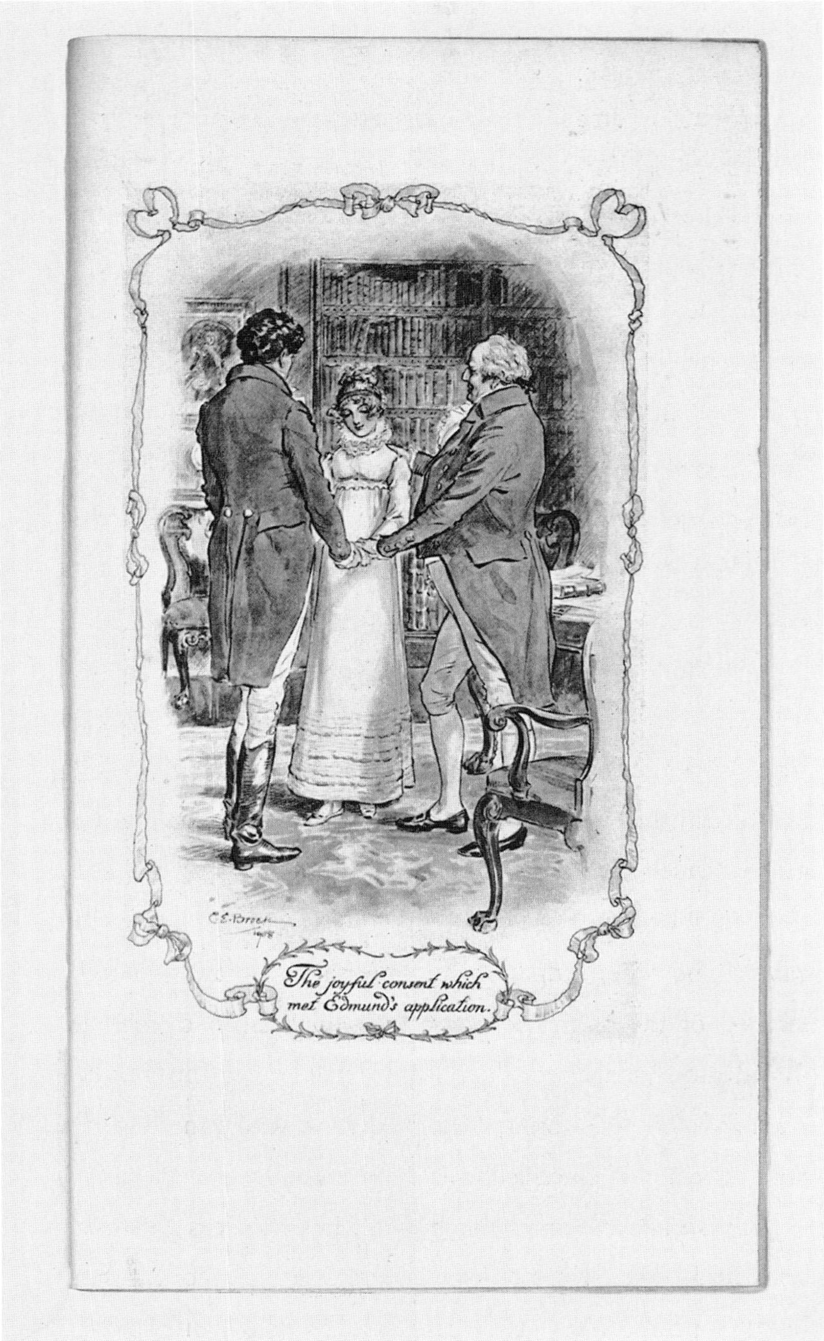
The joyful consent which
met Edmund's application.

Sir Thomas joyfully consents to the marriage of his son Edmund and niece Fanny in this illustration from 1908.

mature woman who had borne sorrow and disappointment. Bright, engaging Elizabeth Bennet belongs to Austen's more carefree past, but the women of *Mansfield Park* are creations of her later years. Mary Crawford possesses Elizabeth's wit and allure, but she never gains self-knowledge. Fanny Price shows good sense, but she is sober and dull. "*Mansfield Park* is altogether an old book," wrote a literary scholar in the late 1800s, "with none of the merit of youth."

The author herself had lost the spring of youth, according to what the novelist Mary Russell Mitford heard from a mutual friend. The friend reported that Austen had "stiffened into the most perpendicular, precise, taciturn piece of 'single blessedness' that ever existed, and that, till *Pride and Prejudice* showed what a precious gem was hidden in that unbending case, she was no more regarded in society than a poker or a fire-screen." Yet Henry Austen described a very different Jane. "Her voice was extremely sweet. She delivered herself with fluency and precision," he observed. "Indeed she was formed for elegant and rational society, excelling in conversation as much as in composition."

Jane made a list of the earliest reactions to *Mansfield Park*. She noted that Cassandra, who was "Fond of Fanny" and "Delighted much in Mr. Rushworth's stupidity," found it "quite clever, tho' not so brilliant as P. & P. [*Pride and Prejudice*]." Mrs. Austen thought Fanny Price was "insipid," but she enjoyed Mrs. Norris. Jane's friend Anne Sharp called the novel "excellent." She noted, "Of it's good sense & moral Tendency there can be no doubt.—

Henry Austen sat for this portrait in his minister's robe. Jane was fondest of this engaging, impulsive brother.

Your Characters are drawn to the Life.—so *very, very* natural & just—but as you beg me to be perfectly honest, I must confess I prefer P & P." Anne had left Godmersham in 1806 to take another position, but she and Jane stayed in touch through letters.

A Mrs. Augusta Bramstone "owned that she thought S & S.—and P. & P. downright nonsense, but expected to like MP. better." Having finished the first volume of *Mansfield Park,* Mrs. Bramstone "flattered herself she had got through the worst."

Another woman, Lady Gordon, captured the essence of Austen's genius:

In most novels you are amused for the time with a set of Ideal People whom you never think of afterwards or whom you the least expect to meet in common life, whereas in Miss A-s works, & especially in M P. you actually live *with them, you fancy yourself one of the family; & the scenes are so exactly descriptive, so perfectly natural, that there is scarcely an Incident or conversation, or a person that you are not inclined to imagine you have at one time or other in your Life been a witness to, born[e] a part in, & been acquainted with.*

The first edition of *Mansfield Park* sold out within six months, but Thomas Egerton refused to print a second one. So Henry Austen offered his sister's next novel to another publisher, John Murray. Murray loved the new book, which was called *Emma,* and bought its copyright. He also purchased the rights to *Sense and Sensibility* and *Mansfield Park,* planning to bring out new editions at a later date.

Jane took over the business negotiations after Henry fell ill. In November 1815, when she went to London to meet with John Murray, Henry was sick enough to need medical care. One of the men treating him was a court physician. This doctor informed the Prince Regent—who admired Austen's books—that the lady novelist was in town. Jane promptly received an invitation from the prince's librarian, the Reverend James Stanier Clarke, to tour the library at Carlton House, the prince's London residence. During this meeting, Clarke hinted that Austen might dedicate her next novel to the prince.

Jane Austen, being no admirer of the Prince Regent, hated

the idea of dedicating her book to him, but a suggestion like this was really a royal command. With no choice but to obey, Austen wrote the briefest dedication possible, one that readers might easily miss: "Emma, Dedicated by Permission to H.R.H. [His Royal Highness] The Prince Regent." Murray told her this would never do. He drafted a proper dedication, one that took up lots of space and befitted a British monarch:

To
His Royal Highness
THE PRINCE REGENT,
this work is,
by His Royal Highness's permission,
most respectfully
dedicated,
by His Royal Highness's
dutiful
and obedient
humble servant,
the author

Murray also produced a scarlet-bound presentation copy of *Emma* for the prince.

The librarian, Clarke, thanked Austen on behalf of His Royal Highness. He then tried to help her by offering a subject for her next novel. He hoped she would describe "the Habits of Life and Character and enthusiasm of a Clergyman"—a man much like himself—"who should pass his time between the metropolis & the Country."

It was a fine notion, but Austen respectfully declined. "Such a man's conversation must at times be on subjects of science and philosophy, of which I know nothing," she tactfully replied. She was, she told Clarke, "the most unlearned and uninformed female who ever dared to be an authoress."

Unwilling to give up his idea, the Reverend Clarke pleaded, "Do let us have an English Clergyman after *your* fancy." Austen might even "Carry your Clergyman to Sea as the Friend of some distinguished Naval Character about a Court." This situation would yield "many interesting Scenes of Character & Interest."

Austen never authored this book, but Clarke did inspire her to write the hilarious "Plan of a Novel, According to Hints from Various Quarters." This imaginary novel features a clergyman, "the most excellent Man that can be imagined, perfect in Character, Temper & Manners." His daughter, too, is faultless, "very highly accomplished, understanding modern Languages & (generally speaking) everything that the most accomplished young Women learn." Father and daughter "converse in long speeches, elegant Language—& a tone of high, serious sentiment." The clergyman tells his daughter about his life, including "his going to sea as a Chaplain to a distinguished Naval Character about the Court, his going afterwards to Court himself, which introduced him to a great variety of Characters."

There was more. After the clergyman is driven from his parish "by the vile arts of some totally unprincipled and heartless young Man," he and his daughter move from country to country. Men fall in love with the daughter wherever she goes, and she receives many proposals of marriage. She also encounters the hero, who is perfect in every way, but who is prevented from addressing her by his high level of refinement. The daughter is repeatedly kidnapped by the villain of the story only to be rescued by her father and the hero, who harbors a secret love for her. She is "often reduced to support herself & her Father by her Talents & work for her Bread;—continually cheated & defrauded of her hire, worn down to a Skeleton, & now & then starved to death."

Father and daughter end up in Kamschatka (the Russian Far East), where the clergyman "after 4 or 5 hours of tender advice & parental Admonition to his miserable Child, expires in a fine burst of Literary Enthusiasm." Then, after "at least 20 narrow escapes," the daughter crawls back to her native land, "runs into the arms of the Hero himself," and, because this is a Jane Austen story, "they are happily united."

Austen displayed her sense of humor again in her fourth published novel, *Emma.*

eight

"IF I LIVE TO BE AN OLD WOMAN..."

There are so many who forget to think
seriously till it is almost too late.

—PERSUASION

WHAT HAPPENS when a young woman claims to act on her intuition but is really guided by a vivid imagination? This question drives the action—and much of the humor—in *Emma.*

In the village of Highbury lives Emma Woodhouse, who is rich, clever, and nearly twenty-one. She shares a fine country home with her father, an aging, worrying hypochondriac. As the story begins, Emma's beloved governess, Miss Taylor, has just married Mr. Weston. More a family friend than an employee, Miss Taylor had let the motherless Emma do pretty much as she liked. "The real evils indeed of Emma's situation were the power of having rather too much of her own way, and a disposition to think a little too well of herself," Austen explained.

One person offers Emma wise guidance, even though she hates to admit that what he says is right. Mr. Knightley is a wealthy neighbor and a friend to both Mr. Woodhouse and Emma.

Emma considers herself an expert in matters of the heart. After all, she correctly predicted that Miss Taylor would marry a neighbor, Mr. Weston (something everyone else had also foreseen). Needing a project, she sets out to find a wife for Mr. Elton, the local minister. She chooses Harriet Smith, a girl born with "the stain of illegitimacy," whose unknown father pays her board at a nearby school. Harriet is sweet and docile rather than clever. She is someone Emma can easily mold and direct.

After Emma persuades Harriet to turn down a marriage proposal from an honest farmer, she finds signs of Mr. Elton's affection for the girl wherever she looks. Mr. Elton wishes to see Emma draw Harriet's likeness—this is one clue. He composes a riddle in verse, the answer to which is courtship—this is another. Mr. Knightley hints that the minister might actually be in love with Emma, and he warns her against encouraging his attention. Emma rejects this foolish notion, expecting that Mr. Elton will soon propose to her friend. When his proposal comes, though, it is addressed not to Harriet, but to Emma. Mr. Knightley was right.

"I see very few pearls in the room except mine"

Mrs. Elton makes sure that people notice her pearls in an illustration from a 1909 edition of *Emma*.

At first Emma is taken aback; then she is furious at being so deceived. Mr. Elton reacts to her unexpected rejection by hurrying away to Bath. He soon returns engaged to someone else, a lady "in possession of an independent fortune, of so many thousands as would always be called ten." Before long, he introduces to Highbury his showy, self-important new wife. "How do you like my gown?—How do you like my trimming?" Mrs. Elton asks, only to claim in the next breath, "Nobody can think less of dress in general than I do."

Someone else also comes to Highbury that year. Frank Churchill is Mr. Weston's son from his first marriage. Years earlier, after his mother died, Frank was adopted by a rich aunt and uncle, much as Edward Austen was adopted by the Knights. The Westons hope for a union between Frank and Emma, but Emma feels no love for this young man. Instead, she thinks that he might be just the right husband for her friend. When Harriet admits to feeling an attachment to a man of higher rank, Emma is sure she means Frank and resolves to see her plan carried out.

Emma herself may not love Frank, but she likes to gossip with him about another girl, Jane Fairfax. Jane is an orphan staying in Highbury with her grandmother and aunt. Miss Bates, Jane's aunt, is a well-meaning chatterbox and a woman who had Austen's sympathy. Miss Bates's "youth had passed without distinction, and her middle life was devoted to the care of a failing mother, and the endeavour to make a small income go as far as possible."

Jane Fairfax is penniless and will soon seek a job as a governess. She is at least Emma's equal in learning and accomplishments and would be a more suitable friend than Harriet Smith. But to befriend Jane might mean confronting her own shortcomings, so Emma has fun at her expense instead.

Frank confides that he has met Jane Fairfax before, and Emma reveals her suspicion that Jane is secretly loved by the new husband of a close friend. There is evidence: someone has anonymously sent Jane a piano. Who else could have surprised her like this?

The people of Highbury gather socially and reveal their fine points and flaws. The Westons host a ball, and at one point in the evening, Harriet Smith is left without a partner. Mr. Elton is free to dance—his wife has partnered with someone else—yet he rudely ignores Harriet. He judges it beneath him to dance with a girl of such murky parentage. Luckily for Harriet, Mr. Knightley steps forward and asks her to dance, revealing his better manners and kind, considerate nature.

Summer comes, and Mr. Knightley invites his neighbors to his estate to pick berries. One thing clouds the happy outing, however. Mrs. Elton has intruded into Jane Fairfax's life and has found a post as governess for her. She won't leave the subject alone and pressures the girl to take the job. Jane, who dreads the day when she must begin supporting herself, leaves the party early.

The next day, the same group ventures to Box Hill, a spot known for its scenic beauty. This time, Emma is the person who behaves badly. She lets Frank Churchill flirt openly with her, and she thoughtlessly insults Miss Bates. Later, Mr. Knightley takes Emma to task for her behavior, and she is ashamed. "Never had she felt so agitated, mortified, grieved, at any circumstance in her life. She was most forcibly struck," Austen wrote. "How could she have been so brutal, so cruel to Miss Bates!"

By recognizing the power of her words to hurt other people, Emma takes a big step toward growing up. Like Elizabeth Bennet, she is learning to know herself and finding the lesson painful. "Emma felt the tears running down her cheeks almost all the way home, without being at any trouble to check them, extraordinary as they were." When the next morning she goes to the Bates home to apologize, she learns that Jane has accepted the position that Mrs. Elton found for her, but the thought of entering the "governess-trade" has made Jane ill.

Then something happens to change Jane's fate. Frank's aunt, Mrs. Churchill, dies, and a private matter becomes public knowledge. Highbury learns that for months, Frank Churchill and Jane Fairfax have been secretly engaged. With his aunt dead, Frank is free to follow his heart and marry Jane. Mrs. Churchill would have opposed the match, but her husband will not.

After marrying off one of Highbury's eligible young women, Jane Austen turned her attention to the other two. Harriet feels no heartbreak upon learning of Frank's engagement, because, as she tells Emma, the gentleman she cares for is Mr.

Knightley. This news troubles Emma; could Mr. Knightley be fond of Harriet, too? "Till now that she was threatened with its loss, Emma had never known how much of her happiness depended on being *first* with Mr. Knightley, first in interest and affection." Acknowledging that it would pain her to see Mr. Knightley attached to another woman, Emma understands that she loves him.

Happily for Emma, Mr. Knightley soon joins her as she walks in the garden. She fears that he will speak of Harriet, but instead he asks Emma to be his wife. As in *Pride and Prejudice,* Austen stepped back at this crucial point in the story, writing, "What did she say?—just what she ought, of course. A lady always does." Readers can only imagine Emma's words of love. Harriet overcomes her regret at not being Mr. Knightley's chosen one and marries the steadfast farmer.

Jane Austen wrote down readers' reactions to *Emma,* just as she had done for *Mansfield Park.* She noted that Cassandra liked the new novel better than *Pride and Prejudice,* but *Mansfield Park* remained her favorite. Mrs. Austen disagreed, calling *Emma* "more entertaining than MP. [*Mansfield Park*]—but not so interesting as P. & P." In Jane's mother's opinion, none of the characters in *Emma* could compare to Lady Catherine de Bourgh and Mr. Collins in *Pride and Prejudice*. Austen's rich aunt and uncle, the Leigh-Perrots, "saw many beauties" in *Emma,* "but could not think it equal to P. & P.—Darcy and Elizabeth had spoilt them for anything else."

Martha Lloyd thought *Emma* "as *clever* as either of the

others, but did not receive so much pleasure from it as from P. & P—& M P." Anne Sharp was "pleased with the Heroine for her Originality," and delighted with Mr. Knightley. She "called Mrs. Elton beyond praise," but felt "dissatisfied with Jane Fairfax."

Fanny Knight "could not bear *Emma* herself." She called Mr. Knightley "delightful" and thought she might like Jane Fairfax if she knew her better. Fanny loaned the novel to a friend, who wrote, "I am at Highbury all day, & I can't help feeling I have just got into a new set of acquaintance."

Jane Austen let her readers imagine her lovers' most tender moments, but viewers of the 1996 film *Emma* saw Emma Woodhouse and Mr. Knightley (Gwyneth Paltrow and Jeremy Northam) marry and kiss.

Austen's friend Martha Lloyd was photographed sometime after 1839. She married in 1828, at age sixty-three, becoming Frank Austen's second wife.

Austen's observant nephew Edward, her brother Edward's oldest son, was quick to point out an error. He noted that Austen had managed to make Mr. Knightley's apple trees bloom several weeks late, on the day of strawberry picking in July.

Sir Walter Scott, the novelist of action and adventure, reviewed *Emma* in 1815. He wrote that in this newest book, as in all her work, "the author displays her peculiar powers of humour and knowledge of human life." She presents "to the reader, instead of the splendid scenes of an imaginary world, a correct and striking representation of that which is daily taking place around him."

Tastes change, and a novelist of a later generation, Anthony Trollope, called *Emma* "very tedious." He found the dialogue too long and sometimes unnecessary. Of Emma herself, he wrote: "Her weaknesses are all plain to us, but of her strength we are only told; and even at the last we hardly know why Mr.

Knightley loves her." Trollope had to admit, though, that the story shows "wonderful knowledge of female character."

After John Murray printed a second edition of *Mansfield Park* in February 1816, Austen finally could afford to send Richard Crosby's firm the ten pounds she had been paid thirteen years earlier for *Susan,* which was never published. Crosby returned it to her, and she went through the manuscript, changing the heroine's name to Catherine. Austen had completed this novel in 1803. Since then she had matured as an author, so for the present, she told Fanny Knight, "Miss Catherine" would remain "upon the Shelve."

Around this time, Austen started to feel ill with mysterious aches and pains. She told herself that nothing was wrong and worked on her newest novel, *The Elliots.* She might as well write: there was no time to be sick when others were dealing with real troubles. Her brother Charles, for instance, was unemployed and struggling to stay out of poverty. Charles had been chasing pirates in the Mediterranean Sea when the vessel he captained was shipwrecked. With Britain finally at peace, he would wait ten years for the navy to offer him another command. Charles was raising three motherless daughters, and the middle child, Harriet, suffered from raging headaches. Doctors were treating the little girl with doses of mercury, a toxic metal. "I hope Heaven in its mercy will take her soon. Her poor Father will be quite worn out by his feelings for her," the child's aunt Jane commented. (Harriet would defy her aunt's cold-hearted wish and live for nearly fifty more years.)

Charles Austen would marry again in 1820, choosing his dead wife's sister as his bride. He would remain in the navy and rise to the rank of rear admiral.

The other naval officer in the family saw his pay cut in half. Frank Austen had made some smart investments and hoped to weather the downturn without too much discomfort. But he had put some of his money into Henry's bank, and in 1816, the bank collapsed. Henry had taken daring risks with his investors' funds, which included thirteen pounds of Jane's earnings from *Mansfield Park*. Such a big gamble was a mistake in this unsettled economic time, and he lost the money. His rich relatives—his brother Edward and uncle Leigh-Perrot—paid out large sums to cover his losses.

Henry's charm melted his family's anger, and those who could afford it helped him along financially. "My uncle had been living for some years past at considerable expense, but not more than might become the head of a flourishing bank," wrote James's daughter Caroline. For this reason, "no blame of personal extravagance was ever imputed to him." Only the Leigh-Perrots refused to forgive him. Henry, cheerful by nature, decided that at last the time had come to be ordained a minister. By the end of the year, he was serving as a curate in Chawton.

Jane might have been content to ignore her health, but Cassandra worried about her. In May and June 1816, Cassandra took Jane to the spa town of Cheltenham. Waters from the mineral springs in Cheltenham, like those in Bath, could restore wellness—or so people thought. Every morning before breakfast, Jane walked to the local pump room and downed a pint of the foul-tasting water. She and Cassandra could only hope that the treatment helped.

Back at home, the sisters often cooked for Frank and his family. They entertained Frank's children, and they kept an eye on Charles's oldest girl, Cassy, who stayed for months at a time with her grandmother and aunts. "Composition seems to me Impossible, with a head full of Joints of Mutton & doses of rhubarb," Jane complained to Cassandra. She wrote anyway, despite the turmoil and a painful back, and inscribed "Finis" on the final page of *The Elliots* on July 18, 1816. Something about the novel's ending bothered her, though, so she rewrote the last two chapters.

And she insisted that she was getting better. In January 1817, she claimed to be "stronger than I was half a year ago." She informed Alethea Bigg that the problem was *"Bile,"* but she told her niece Fanny that she was bothered by rheumatism,

Frank Austen attained the highest rank in the Royal Navy, admiral of the fleet, and was knighted by King William IV in 1837.

which was almost better, "just a little pain in my knee now & then." She was also "recovering my Looks a little, which have been bad enough, black & white & every wrong colour." Jane Austen fought hard against being ill, believing that "Sickness is a dangerous Indulgence at my time of Life." She was forty-one years old.

She hated being treated like an invalid, too. If she felt tired after dinner, she lined up three parlor chairs and lay across the seats, leaving the sofa for her mother, who sometimes napped there. The chair arrangement "never looked comfortable," Caroline Austen said. "I often asked her how she *could* like the chairs best—and I suppose I worried her into telling me the reason of her choice—which was, that if she ever used the sofa, Grandmama would be leaving it for her, and would not lie down, as she did now, whenever she felt inclined."

Austen began another novel, one she called *The Brothers*. It concerned three or four families, the mix of characters she liked best. Instead of living in a country village, they inhabited Sanditon, an up-and-coming seaside resort. She had written twelve chapters by March, but then she put the manuscript aside, feeling too ill to write anything longer than a letter.

This sounds like the behavior of a very sick woman. Yet when her uncle Leigh-Perrot died, on March 28, at age eighty-two, Jane insisted that Cassandra leave her and go to Berkshire, to be with their newly widowed aunt. All the Austens waited eagerly to learn the contents of the old man's will, but its reading let them down. Mr. Leigh-Perrot left six thousand pounds in a trust fund for James, the oldest of the Austen brothers. He left a thousand pounds to each of his other nephews and nieces (except the disabled George), but this money was to be disbursed at the time of their aunt's death. They had expected much more, and certainly, as the dead man's sister, Jane's mother had counted on getting some money to live on. She received nothing. Jane took a turn for the worse and blamed it on this distressing news. She summoned Cassandra home.

Caroline and Anna called at Chawton Cottage around this time. When they entered their aunt Jane's room, they saw her wearing a dressing gown and seated "quite like an invalide in an arm chair," Caroline reported. "I was struck by the alteration in herself—She was very pale—her voice was weak and low and there was about her, a general appearance of debility and suffering." Her nieces kept the visit short, because Austen was too weak to talk. "I do not suppose we stayed a quarter of an hour; and *I* never saw Aunt Jane again," Caroline said.

Jane was so sick in April, with a fever and "discharge," that her alarmed family brought in Mr. Lyford, a surgeon from Winchester. This medical man applied treatments that Jane said "gradually removed the Evil." She knew that her condition was grave, though. Secretly, on April 27, she wrote a will, bequeathing "to my dearest Sister Cassandra Elizabeth everything of which I may die possessed, or which may be hereafter due to me." Funeral expenses were to be deducted from the total as well as fifty pounds for her beloved brother Henry and fifty more for Madame Bigeon, a longtime servant in Henry's home. Madame Bigeon had looked after young Hastings, nursed Eliza in her final illness, and lost her savings when Henry's bank fell.

No longer fighting the notion of being sick, Jane agreed to go to Winchester to be under Lyford's constant care. James and Mary Lloyd Austen loaned her their carriage. "Now, that's the sort of thing which Mrs. J. Austen does in the kindest manner!" Jane said. "But still," she added, "she is in the main *not* a liberal-minded Woman." She had never warmed to James's second wife.

Jane and Cassandra left Chawton on May 24, a rainy day. Henry Austen and a nephew, William Knight, traveled beside the carriage on horseback, and Jane worried about them getting wet. She felt grateful for her family's attention. "If I live to be an old Woman I must expect to wish I had died now, blessed in the tenderness of such a Family," she wrote in a letter to

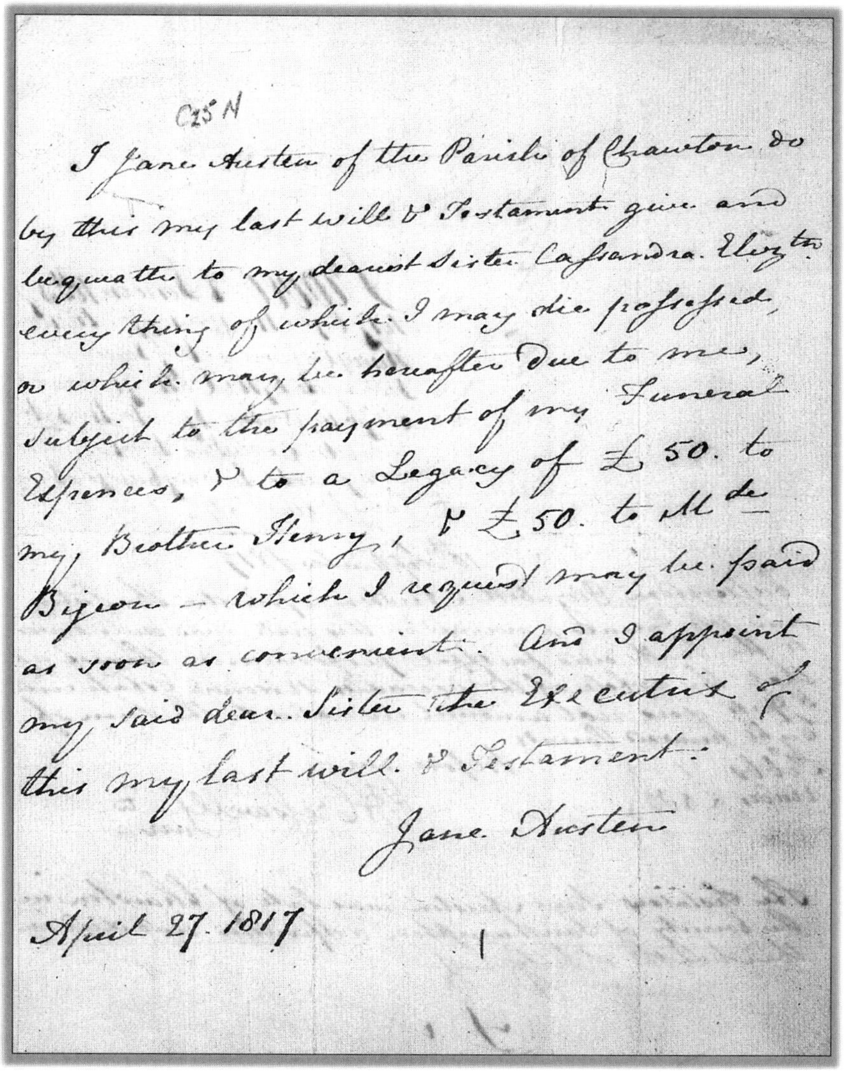

C25 N

I Jane Austen of the Parish of Chawton do
by this my last Will & Testament give and
bequeath to my dearest Sister Cassandra Elizth
every thing of which I may die possessed,
or which may be hereafter due to me,
subject to the payment of my Funeral
Expences, & to a Legacy of £50. to
my Brother Henry, & £50. to Mde
Bijion — which I request may be paid
as soon as convenient. And I appoint
my said dear Sister the Executrix of
this my last Will & Testament.

Jane Austen

April 27. 1817

Jane Austen drafted her will secretly, leaving almost everything she possessed to Cassandra.

Anne Sharp. "Sick or Well, beleive me ever yr attached friend." Sharp kept this letter close to her heart for the rest of her life.

What ailed Jane Austen? Doctors and historians can only guess. One condition that fits her symptoms is Addison's disease, possibly brought on by tuberculosis. In Addison's disease, the adrenal glands produce too little of certain hormones that the body needs to function. Patients feel weak and tired, fevers come and go, and dark blotches appear on the skin. People with Addison's disease feel some aches, especially in the lower back, but the pain is milder than that of cancer. Today, patients take medication to replace the missing hormones, but in Austen's time their condition had no name and no treatment. Doctors had no tests to detect the "Addisonian crisis"—the lethal combination of low blood pressure, a low blood level of sugar, and a high blood level of potassium—that took the patient's life. It is possible, however, that Austen had a different illness. Some medical detectives have suggested that she suffered from uncomplicated tuberculosis or lymphoma (cancer beginning in the lymph nodes).

In Winchester, the sisters rented rooms one floor above street level at Number 8, College Street. From their bow window, they looked out on the old city wall. Jane told Cassandra that she was getting better, and to prove it she walked from room to room. Cassandra saw things differently, and wrote to Mary Lloyd Austen in Steventon, asking her to come and help with Jane's care. Mary arrived on June 6, a Friday.

Mary Austen kept a diary, and on Sunday, June 8, she noted

that she "stay'd with Jane whilst Cass went to Church." On Monday, she wrote, "Jane Austen worse I sat up with her." And on Tuesday, "Jane in great danger." News of Jane's decline reached the rest of the family. "We can no longer flatter ourselves with the least hope of having your dear valuable Aunt Jane restored to us," James Austen wrote to his son, then a student at Oxford. "Your grandmamma has suffered much; but her affliction can be nothing to Cassandra's."

Then Jane surprised them all and seemed to rally. Mary, no longer needed, went home, but within days, she came back. Cassandra and Jane required her help again.

nine

LASTING WORDS

There is no charm equal to tenderness of heart.

—Emma

On July 15, St. Swithin's Day, the women on College Street woke up to rain. According to English tradition, rain on this date means that wet weather will linger for forty days. On this particular July 15, the people of Winchester hoped for sun, because they had scheduled a day of races. In her mind, Jane composed a poem, imagining Saint Swithin cursing Winchester's citizens for holding races on his special day. Too weak to hold a pen, she recited the verses aloud, and Cassandra wrote them down:

These races & revels & dissolute measures
With which you're debasing a neighbouring Plain

Let them stand—you shall meet with your curse in
your pleasures
Set off for your course, I'll pursue with my *rain.*

Inventing this poem used up the last drops of Jane's strength. She grew weaker and sicker, until on the afternoon of July 17, Lyford gave her something strong to ease her pain. It was the end; she died in her sister's arms before the next sunrise. On July 18, Mary wrote in her diary, "Jane breathed her last 1/2 after four in the Morn."

Cassandra closed the eyes of the sister who had been her best friend. "She was the sun of my life, the gilder of every pleasure, the soother of every sorrow," Cassandra mourned; "it is as if I had lost a part of myself." For six days, the body lay in its open coffin in one of the College Street rooms. On July 24, Jane Austen was buried in a brick-lined vault in Winchester Cathedral, the city's ancient, historic church. Three of Jane's brothers—Henry, Edward, and Francis—and one of her nephews—James Edward—attended.

Illness kept James in Steventon, but he penned a rhyming tribute to the sister he had lost:

In her (rare union) were combined
A fair form & a fairer mind;
Hers, Fancy quick & clear good sense
And wit which never gave offence . . .

Jane Austen was laid to rest within Winchester Cathedral.

James claimed that his sister always used her wit kindly, but he may have been less than honest. A few lines later, he contradicted himself by mentioning Jane's "quick & keen . . . mental eye," which "seemed for ever on the watch, / Some traits of ridicule to catch."

The Reverend Henry Austen wrote the inscription carved in his sister's black marble gravestone. He praised "the benevolence of her heart, the sweetness of her temper, and the extraordinary endowments of her mind," but he mentioned nothing about her writing. Henry, like the rest of his family, had no idea that with her novels, Jane had placed herself among the world's great writers.

Henry lost the letters he received from Jane, or possibly he destroyed them, just as Cassandra burned so many of hers. Frank Austen carefully saved his letters from Jane, but when he died in 1865, his daughter Frances threw them away. Jane Austen wrote about three thousand letters, but only one hundred sixty survive.

She also completed two novels that were unpublished at the time of her death. They appeared in print together in December 1817. The first was *Catherine* (formerly *Susan*), which had come off the shelf and had a new title, *Northanger Abbey.* Completed in 1803, it brings to mind the broad humor of Austen's Juvenilia as it spoofs the gothic novels that were popular when she was young.

Its heroine, Catherine Morland, is an unlikely one, the daughter of a respectable clergyman with a good income and his sensible wife. Catherine's father is "not in the least addicted to locking up his daughters," and her mother, rather than dying in childbirth "as anybody might expect," lives on. "Almost pretty" at seventeen, Catherine is an ordinary girl.

Her life becomes an adventure when a neighbor couple, the Allens, take Catherine to Bath. There, at a ball, she dances with "a very gentleman-like" young clergyman named Henry Tilney. The next day, she meets Isabella Thorpe, the daughter of Mrs. Allen's old friend. The two girls quickly become close companions. They share a taste for gothic romances, and Catherine reads *The Mysteries of Udolpho,* which Isabella praises. This novel by Ann Radcliffe focuses

Women find thrills in a gothic novel in 1802.

on a beautiful orphan who has frightening experiences in a foreign castle.

Catherine hopes to see Henry Tilney again, but Isabella's tiresome brother, John, gets in the way. John has formed the mistaken idea that Catherine is an heiress, and he is determined to court her. Catherine at last speaks with Henry and meets his sister, Eleanor, and his father, General Tilney. Calling Catherine "the finest girl in Bath," the general invites her to stay with his family at their home, Northanger Abbey.

Northanger Abbey! The name makes Catherine imagine "a fine old place, just like what one reads about," a spot like the castle of Udolpho. She thinks of dim, gloomy passages; hidden doorways; and rooms that have been closed since their inhabitants' deaths. When she sees Northanger Abbey's modern furnishings and brightly lit rooms, she is disappointed.

Her bed chamber is clean and sunny, but an antique chest promises to hold forbidden secrets. Curiosity impels Catherine to raise its lid, and she discovers—a spare counterpane, or bedspread. Catherine's fancy targets General Tilney, and she con-

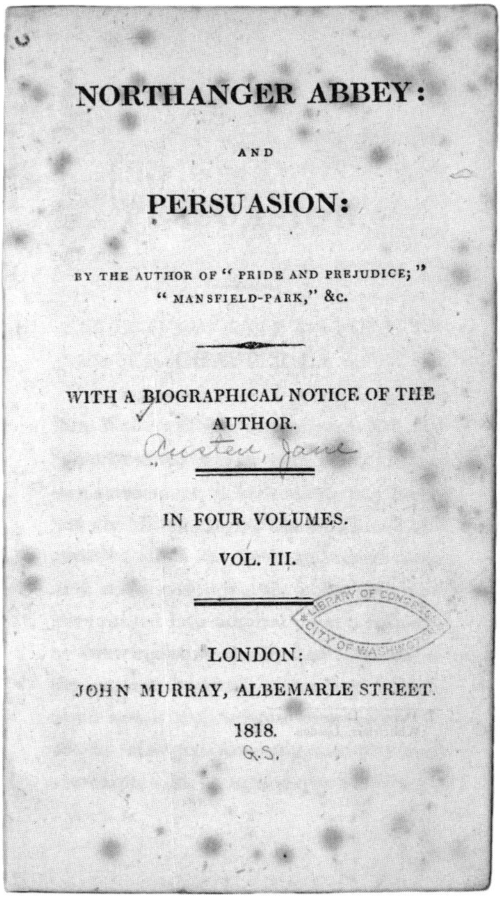
NORTHANGER ABBEY:

AND

PERSUASION:

BY THE AUTHOR OF "PRIDE AND PREJUDICE;" "MANSFIELD-PARK," &c.

WITH A BIOGRAPHICAL NOTICE OF THE AUTHOR.

Austen, Jane

IN FOUR VOLUMES.

VOL. III.

LONDON:

JOHN MURRAY, ALBEMARLE STREET.

1818.

G.S.

John Murray published *Northanger Abbey* and *Persuasion* together in a four-volume set dated 1818, although the books were printed in December 1817.

Stylish Britons stroll outside Bath's pump room in 1804.

jures up "the blackest suspicions" that he murdered his wife. The hunt for clues leads her to the late Mrs. Tilney's room, where Henry catches her snooping. "Dear Miss Morland, consider the dreadful nature of the suspicions you have entertained," Henry chides, and Catherine, embarrassed, hurries to her room in tears.

This is the painful lesson in self-knowledge that causes Catherine to grow: "The visions of romance were over. Catherine was completely awakened. Henry's address, short as it had been, had more thoroughly opened her eyes to the extravagance of her late fancies than all their several disappointments had done."

There is a surprise in store for Catherine at Northanger

Abbey, but it is nothing she could have imagined. General Tilney returns from a week in London and orders her to leave, offering no explanation. A perplexed Catherine journeys home alone and reaches her family safely. The reason for the general's unexpected anger becomes clear when Henry pays a call. He explains that in Bath, General Tilney had learned from Isabella's brother, John Thorpe, that Catherine was to inherit a great deal of money, and the general had picked Catherine out as a wife for Henry. Then, in London, John Thorpe had told General Tilney a different story, that Catherine was penniless.

Catherine, in truth, is neither rich nor poor, and Henry asks for her hand in marriage. The Morlands give their permission on the condition that General Tilney agrees to the match. Fortunately for Catherine and Henry, Eleanor Tilney marries a viscount, "a man of fortune and consequence," and the general feels happy and forgiving. He grants Henry permission "to be a fool if he liked it!"

Northanger Abbey is Catherine Morland's story, but it is a book about novels and reading as well. Austen may poke fun at thrillers like *The Mysteries of Udolpho,* which were written for popular entertainment, but in *Northanger Abbey* she also defends the novel as an art form:

There seems almost a general wish of decrying the capacity and undervaluing the labour of the novelist, and of slighting the performances which have only genius, wit, and taste to recommend them. . . . "And what are you reading, Miss—?" "Oh! It is

What was an abbey? In the 1500s, King Henry VIII abolished the monasteries in his domain. A number of the abbeys, or monks' residences, became homes for the wealthy. In Austen's time, some rich Britons also built new homes in the style of the old abbeys. Perhaps the grandest was Fonthill Abbey, completed in 1813. This view of Fonthill Abbey's western hall shows how forbidding these houses could feel.

only a novel!" . . . or, in short, only some work in which the greatest powers of the mind are displayed, in which the most thorough knowledge of human nature, the happiest delineation of its varieties, the liveliest effusions of wit and humour, are conveyed to the world in the best-chosen language.

This is Jane Austen, age twenty-two, speaking across the centuries about a subject close to her heart.

The second of the two novels published after Austen's death was the last one she finished. She had called it *The Elliots*, but in print it bore the title *Persuasion*. It offers the most seasoned outlook of all Austen's novels and features her oldest heroine.

Anne Elliot is twenty-seven and single when the story begins. Eight years earlier, she was engaged to marry a young naval officer named Frederick Wentworth, but she was persuaded to break the engagement by Lady Russell, a good friend of Anne's late mother who has grown close to Anne. At the time, Wentworth had no money and an uncertain future, so Lady Russell believed that she gave good advice. Wentworth left, "feeling himself ill-used by so forced a relinquishment." For Anne, who had loved him, the "attachment and regrets had, for a long time, clouded every enjoyment of youth, and an early loss of bloom and spirits had been their lasting effect." She has since put aside any hope of marriage.

Whatever Anne's father and sisters knew of this brief engagement has been forgotten. Anne "was nobody with either

Anne Elliot (played by Amanda Root) and Captain Wentworth (Ciarán Hinds) come face to face over the fallen form of Louisa Musgrove in the 1995 film *Persuasion.* Wentworth's friend Captain Benwick (Richard McCabe) stands at the center.

father or sister; her word had no weight, her convenience was always to give way—she was only Anne." Her father, Sir Walter Elliot, basks in the glow of his illustrious family history. He admires his own good looks and his fine home, Kellynch Hall. Anne's older sister, Elizabeth, is as proud and haughty as their father. Her younger sister, Mary, is married to a man named Charles Musgrove and has two children. Mary is a lazy woman who complains about her health. She takes advantage of Anne's willingness to care for her. Single and nearly past the age for marriage, Anne bows to others' wishes and needs.

Debts force Sir Walter to rent Kellynch Hall. His tenants

turn out to be Admiral Croft and his wife, who is Captain Wentworth's sister. Sir Walter and Elizabeth go to live in Bath, but Anne remains behind to visit Mary. Anne knows that with the Crofts living in the neighborhood, she will see Captain Wentworth again before long. The meeting, which Anne both dreads and hopes for, takes place when he comes to stay with the Crofts and calls on the extended Musgrove family. Wentworth, too, has remained single, but he has made a success of himself and is ready to find a wife. It pains Anne to have him treat her with cold politeness while he pays attention to Mary's sister-in-law Louisa Musgrove.

Both Anne and Captain Wentworth are part of a group that makes an overnight excursion to the seashore at Lyme. As Anne begins to wonder if Wentworth might still have feelings for her, an accident mars the happy outing. Louisa Musgrove jumps from the high seawall that runs along the beach. She expects Wentworth to catch her, but she falls and hits her head. In the confusion of the moment, as some people swoon and cry, and the rest try to think what to do, Anne takes charge, overseeing Louisa's immediate care. Her good sense and natural leadership are not lost on Captain Wentworth. He remains near Louisa during her long recovery, but as she gets well, Louisa forms an attachment to another naval man, Captain Benwick, and consents to marry him. What can this mean for Anne?

She soon has her answer. Anne next encounters Captain Wentworth in Bath. There, he overhears her tell a companion,

"All the privilege I claim for my own sex . . . is that of loving longest, when existence or when hope is gone." Her words have meaning for Wentworth, and he responds by handing her a letter. "Dare not say that man forgets sooner than woman, that his love has an earlier death," Anne reads. "I have loved none but you."

In the five earlier novels, Austen stepped back from her lovers as soon as their path to matrimony was clear. *Persuasion* differs, because both its author and its heroine are older and wiser. Austen lingered with Anne Elliot and Captain Wentworth as they recaptured past happiness and opened their hearts to each other.

"When any two young people take it into their heads to marry," Austen concluded, "they are pretty sure by perseverance to carry their point, be they ever so poor, or ever so imprudent, or ever so little likely to be necessary to each other's ultimate comfort." Anne Elliot and Captain Wentworth are none of the above, possessing "maturity of mind, consciousness of right, and one independent fortune between them." Anne finds happiness as a sailor's wife, with "dread of a future war all that could dim her sunshine."

Having been wrongly persuaded in her youth to give up the man she cared for, Anne Elliot knows how precious young love is. "How eloquent could Anne Elliot have been," Austen wrote, "how eloquent, at least, were her wishes on the side of early warm attachment, and a cheerful confidence in futurity, against that over-anxious caution which seems to insult

Wentworth places his declaration of love before Anne in an illustration from 1909.

exertion and distrust Providence!—She had been forced into prudence in her youth, she learned romance as she grew older—the natural sequel of an unnatural beginning." Cassandra Austen had the final word. Next to this passage in her copy of *Persuasion,* she jotted, "Dear, dear Jane! This deserves to be written in letters of gold."

Afterword

OUR OWN JANE AUSTEN

The person, be it gentleman or lady, who has not pleasure in a good novel, must be intolerably stupid.

—Northanger Abbey

As THE nineteenth century progressed, the bold novels of Charles Dickens, Charlotte Brontë, and other great writers of the Victorian era drowned out Jane Austen's quiet voice. Although French editions of her books appeared within a decade of her death, Austen had only a small but loyal group of admirers. The number of people who had known her in life dwindled as time passed, and in 1865, her last surviving sibling, Frank Austen, died at the great age of ninety-one.

In 1870, her brother James's son, James Edward Austen-Leigh, published *A Memoir of Jane Austen,* the first biography of his esteemed aunt. He based it on the family's fondest recollections and the letters that were allowed to survive. "However little I may have to tell, no one else is left who could tell so much of her," Austen-Leigh wrote. This book ignited public interest in Jane Austen that has never stopped growing. Many editions of her novels have been published since it appeared, in English and other languages.

Some readers find that Austen's novels touch their deepest emotions. They may return to her novels throughout their lives and come to think of Elizabeth Bennet, Emma Woodhouse, and Austen's other memorable characters as people they know. Many revere the novelist herself; in 1894, a British critic coined the term *Janites* (often spelled Janeites), to describe Austen's most devoted fans. The attachment only grew. As decades passed, new generations of readers seemed to feel closer to Austen than the ones before them. This curious fact prompted another man of letters to remark in 1927 that "she has ceased to be the 'Miss Austen' of our parents and become our own 'Jane Austen' or even 'Jane.'"

In 1924, the British writer Rudyard Kipling published a short story titled "The Janeites" about a World War I artillery company whose members found strength and comfort in Austen's novels. As one of the men explains, "There's no one to touch Jane when you're in a tight place." To the soldiers, Austen's characters represented the people and nation that they were defending.

By 1940, Great Britain was fighting another world war. German bombs fell on England's airfields and cities as an enemy once again threatened the British way of life. In that year, some of Austen's admirers optimistically founded the Jane Austen Society of the United Kingdom to buy and restore Chawton Cottage, her final home. Today its members further the study and appreciation of her life and work. They acquire and preserve letters and possessions of the Austen family, and they help maintain Chawton Cottage, which is now a museum. Similarly, the Jane Austen Society of North America and the Jane Austen Society of Australia promote awareness of Austen's novels on their respective continents.

Thousands of Austen's devotees journey to Steventon, Bath, Chawton, and Winchester because they feel close to the author in the places where she lived and died. Austen artifacts have drawing power as well: In 2009 and 2010, crowds of fans flocked to "A Woman's Wit: Jane Austen's Life and Legacy," an exhibit at the Morgan Library & Museum in New York City. The library offered the public a chance to view some of the author's rarely seen letters and manuscripts, as well as drawings, prints, and old books that reflected life in Austen's time.

Many writers have found inspiration for their own work in Austen's books and characters. They have written sequels to her novels and even a mystery series with Mr. and Mrs. Darcy as sleuths. Author Anne Telscombe wrote an ending to the unfinished novel *Sanditon* for a version that was published in 1975. Austen's novels have also been the subjects of parodies, including Seth Grahame-Smith's 2009 bestseller *Pride and Prejudice and Zombies,* in which the undead overrun England. In this book, Elizabeth and Darcy live happily ever after as a zombie-slaying duo.

Jane Austen's novels have inspired plays, radio dramatizations, films, and other productions. Since the release of 1940's *Pride and Prejudice,* the first motion picture based on an Austen novel, there have been more than thirty film and television productions of her books. Also, the 2007 film *Becoming Jane* presented a fictionalized account of Austen's romance with Tom Lefroy. It starred Anne Hathaway as the youthful Jane Austen.

Austen's true-to-life characters and her insights into human nature ensure that her books will never go out of style. Human beings will feel the pressures that weigh on her characters as

Jane Austen's *Emma* inspired the 1995 film *Clueless,* in which Alicia Silverstone (center) plays a privileged Beverly Hills teen who tries to transform a clueless new classmate into a popular girl.

long as they live in families and communities. Problems will arise as long as couples fall in love and marry. In every generation, young people long to plunge headfirst into life while their elders urge caution, as in *Persuasion*. Women and men fall for good-looking charmers who break their hearts, as in *Sense and Sensibility*. Like Emma, the youthful discover upon reaching adulthood that they understand less than they thought they did. Growing up involves pain, as Austen demonstrated in every one of her novels.

Jane Austen opened new territory for novelists (and filmmakers) by writing about ordinary people and things that happen every day. There will always be an audience for stories about adventures in far-off places or strange doings in frightening castles, but Austen proved that drama can be found in the interactions that take place all around us. "Nothing very much happens in her books, and yet, when you come to the bottom of a page, you eagerly turn it to learn what will happen next. Nothing very much does and again you eagerly turn the page," observed the twentieth-century novelist and playwright W. Somerset Maugham. "The novelist who has the power to achieve this has the most precious gift a novelist can possess."

Notes

All books and articles cited in the notes are listed in the bibliography.

p. xi Austen, "I cannot anyhow . . ." is from Le Faye 1995, p. 86.

One: Gentle Aunt Jane?

p. 1 Austen, "Now be sincere . . ." is from J. Austen, *Pride and Prejudice,* p. 248.

p. 3 "fine naturally curling hair . . ." is from Le Faye 1988, p. 419.

p. 3 "long, long black hair . . ." is quoted in Tomalin, p. 110.

p. 3 "two of the prettiest girls . . ." is quoted in William and Richard Arthur Austen-Leigh 1913, p. 61.

p. 3 "of being a decidedly handsome woman," is from Le Faye 1988, p. 419.

p. 5 James Edward Austen-Leigh, "Her sweetness . . ." is from James Edward Austen-Leigh, p. 165.

p. 5 Henry Austen, "Faultless herself . . ." is quoted in Chapman 1949, pp. 95–96.

p. 5 "I do not suppose . . ." is quoted in William and Richard Arthur Austen-Leigh 1913, p. 240.

p. 5 Austen, "I do not want People . . ." is from Le Faye 1995, p. 29.

p. 5 Austen, "For what do we live . . ." is from J. Austen, *Pride and Prejudice*, p. 237.

p. 5 Austen, "Mrs. Allen was one of that numerous class . . ." is from J. Austen, *Northanger Abbey*, p. 10.

p. 7 Austen, "little bit (two inches wide) . . ." is quoted in Tomalin, p. 261.

p. 7 James, "little touches of human truth . . ." is quoted in Bloom 1986, p. 72.

p. 10 Austen, "Single Women have a dreadful propensity . . ." is from Le Faye 1995, p. 332.

p. 10 Austen, "the delight of my life . . ." is from Le Faye 1995, p. 275.

Two: The Novelist Is Born

p. 11 Austen, "My conduct must tell you . . ." is from J. Austen, *The Watsons*, p. 256.

p. 11 George Austen, "Last night the time came . . ." is from Richard A. Austen-Leigh, pp. 82–83.

p. 13 "a profound scholar . . ." is quoted in William and Richard Arthur Austen-Leigh 1913, p. 23.

p. 15 "seem to have no object . . ." is from *The Habits of Good Society*, p. 24.

p. 20 "Tilts and Tournaments . . ." is from Francklin, unnumbered page.

p. 21 "To speak with elegance . . ." is quoted in Nokes, p. 78.

p. 21 Cassandra Leigh Austen, "If Cassandra's head . . ." is quoted in Le Faye 1988, p. 420.

p. 21 Swift, "reading books, except those of devotion . . ." is from Swift, pp. 282–283.

p. 24 Austen, "where young ladies for enormous pay . . ." is from J. Austen, *Emma,* p. 12.

p. 25 de Feuillide, "notwithstanding my reluctance . . ." is quoted in Le Faye 2002, p. 71.

p. 25 de Feuillide, "still my Heart gives the preference . . ." is quoted in Le Faye 2002, p. 116.

p. 26 Austen, "If a book is well written . . ." is from J. Austen, *Catharine and Other Writings,* p. 192.

p. 26 "every circumstance . . ." is quoted in Nokes, p. 108.

p. 26 Burney, "The whole of this unfortunate business . . ." is from Burney, p. 930.

p. 27 Brunton, "glide through the world . . ." is quoted in Elwood, p. 216.

p. 27 Wollstonecraft, "The minds of women . . ." is from Wollstonecraft, p. 2.

p. 28 Sentiment, "not one Eastern Tale . . ." and "no love, and no lady . . ." are from Mack, p. 52.

p. 28 Sentiment, "some nice affecting stories . . ." is from Mack, p. 53.

p. 28 Austen, "Beware of fainting-fits . . ." is from Beer, p. 122.

p. 30 Walter, "not at all pretty . . ." through "was not so well pleased . . ." is quoted in Le Faye 2002, pp. 86–87.

p. 30 Austen, "envious, spiteful, and malicious," and "of so dazzling a beauty . . ." are from Beer, p. 47.

p. 30 George Austen, "You may either by a contemptuous . . ." is quoted in Tomalin, p. 63.

p. 32 Austen, "Oh, what a Henry!" is from Woolsey, p. 255.

p. 32 Austen, "Henry Frederic Howard Fitzwilliam . . ." is quoted in Norman, p. 47.

Three: Love and Losses

p. 33 Austen, "I am almost afraid . . ." is from Chapman 1952, pp. 1–2.

p. 33 de Feuillide, "greatly improved . . ." is quoted in Le Faye 2002, p. 116.

pp. 33,35 "a good deal of color . . ." and "very lively . . ." are from "Letters to the Editor: Jane Austen," p. 591.

p. 35 "a tall thin *spare* person . . ." and "great colour . . ." are from Le Faye 1985, p. 495.

p. 35 "full round cheeks . . ." is from James Edward Austen-Leigh, p. 82.

p. 35 "tall & slight . . ." is quoted in Le Faye 1988, p. 418.

p. 35 "rather tall and slender . . ." is from James Edward Austen-Leigh, p. 82.

p. 35 "She was fond of . . ." is from Henry Austen, p. xi.

p. 37 "animated atoms," is quoted in Hopkins, p. 10.

p. 38 Austen, "everything most profligate . . ." is from Chapman 1952, p. 2.

p. 39 Austen, "I shall refuse him . . ." is from Chapman 1952, p. 5.

p. 40 Lefroy, "boyish love," is quoted in Chapman 1949, p. 58.

p. 41 Blackall, "the hope of creating . . ." is quoted in Chapman 1952, p. 28.

p. 41 Austen, "And it is therefore most probable . . ." and "Perhaps she thinks . . ." are from Chapman 1952, p. 28.

p. 41 Austen, "a piece of Perfection . . ." is from Chapman 1952, p. 317.

p. 42 Cadell, "Declined by Return of Post," is quoted in Tomalin, p. 214.

p. 43 de Feuillide, "alas instead of his . . ." and "Jane says that her sister behaves . . ." are from Richard A. Austen-Leigh, p. 159.

p. 44 de Feuillide, "the unspeakable happiness . . ." is from Le Faye 2002, p. 100.

p. 45 Walter, "Poor Eliza must be left . . ." is quoted in Le Faye 1979, p. 14.

p. 46 "dear little Boy," is from Richard A. Austen-Leigh, p. 136.

p. 47 de Feuillide, "dear Liberty . . ." is from Richard A. Austen-Leigh, p. 156.

p. 47 de Feuillide, "the excellence of his Heart . . ." is from Richard A. Austen-Leigh, p. 168.

p. 47 Cassandra Leigh Austen, "you, my dear Mary . . ." is from Richard A. Austen-Leigh, p. 228.

p. 47 Eliza Austen, "very sensible . . ." is from Richard A. Austen-Leigh, p. 157.

p. 48 Anna Austen, "the common-looking carpet . . ." is quoted in Tomalin, p. 108.

p. 49 Anna Austen, "I made it a pleasure . . ." is from Le Faye 1988, p. 418.

Four: Uprooted

p. 50 Austen, "I consider everybody . . ." is from Le Faye 1995, p. 159.

p. 52 Leigh-Perrot, "To have two Young Creatures . . ." is quoted in William and Richard Arthur Austen-Leigh 1989, p. 109.

p. 53 Austen, "two very nice sized rooms . . ." is from Le Faye 1995, p. 40.

p. 53 Austen, "have more than its' usual charm . . ." is from Le Faye 1995, p. 43.

p. 54 Austen, "appeared exactly as she did . . ." is quoted in Le Faye 1995, p. 61.

p. 55 "the girls," is from Le Faye 1988, p. 144.

p. 56 Austen, "We have lived long enough . . ." is from Le Faye 1995, p. 68.

p. 57 Austen, "The whole World is in a conspiracy . . ." is from Le Faye 1995, p. 88.

p. 57 Austen, "has not had the patience . . ." and "as I do not chuse . . ." are from Le Faye 1995, p. 71.

p. 58 Austen, "vapour, shadow, smoke & confusion," is from Le Faye 1995, p. 82.

p. 58 Austen, "like any other short girl . . ." is from Le Faye 1995, p. 86.

p. 60 Anna Austen, "the short Holyday . . ." is quoted in William and Richard Arthur Austen-Leigh 1989, p. 120.

p. 61 Henry Austen, "the Temple of delight," is quoted in Tomalin, p. 136.

p. 61 de Feuillide, "So awful a dissolution . . ." is quoted in Le Faye 1979, p. 13.

p. 63 Anna Austen, "A little talent . . ." is quoted in Le Faye 1988, p. 419.

p. 63 Fanny Knight, "was not so *refined* . . ." is quoted in William and Richard Arthur Austen-Leigh 1989, p. 252.

p. 64 Austen, "They came, and they sat . . ." is from Woolsey, p. 243.

p. 64 "years of chilly solitude . . ." is from "*Vanity Fair*—and *Jane Eyre*," p. 178.

p. 66 Emma Watson [Austen], "Poverty is a great Evil . . ." is from J. Austen, *The Watsons,* p. 255.

p. 66 Elizabeth Watson [Austen], "I think I could like . . ." is from J. Austen, *The Watsons,* p. 256.

p. 67 Austen, "Angelic Woman," "as she used to be," and "Her looks of eager Love . . ." are from Selwyn, pp. 8–9.

p. 68 Austen, "oppression in the head . . ." and "Being quite insensible . . ." are from Le Faye 1995, p. 96.

p. 68 Austen, "The Serenity of the Corpse . . ." is from Le Faye 1995, p. 98.

Five: An Extraordinary Fate

p. 69 Austen, "Let other pens dwell on guilt and misery . . ." is from J. Austen, *Mansfield Park,* p. 312.

p. 69 Austen, "Seven years I suppose . . ." is from Chapman 1952, p. 148.

p. 71 Austen, "His chat seems all forced . . ." is from Chapman 1952, p. 181.

p. 73 Austen, "Till I have a travelling purse . . ." is from Le Faye 1995, p. 135.

p. 73 Austen, "solid principles . . ." is from Le Faye 1995, p. 147.

p. 73 Austen, "dearest Edward . . ." is from Chapman 1952, p. 219.

p. 73 Austen, "I suppose you see . . ." is from Le Faye 1995, p. 137.

p. 73 Caroline Austen, "Her charm to children . . ." and "She would tell us . . ." are quoted in William and Richard Arthur Austen-Leigh 1989, p. 157.

p. 74 Caroline Austen, "She would furnish us . . ." is quoted in James Edward Austen-Leigh, p. 56.

p. 74 Caroline Austen, "the awful stillness . . ." is quoted in Halperin, p. 183.

p. 75 Caroline Austen, "Such was the custom . . ." is quoted in Halperin, p. 186.

p. 76 James Edward Austen-Leigh, "often served for her amusement," and "was as far as possible . . ." from James Edward Austen-Leigh, pp. 87–88.

p. 78 Austen, "I can no more forget it . . ." is from Le Faye 1995, p. 182.

p. 78 Austen, "strength of understanding . . ." is from J. Austen, *Sense and Sensibility,* p. 8.

p. 78 Austen, "eager in every thing . . ." is from J. Austen, *Sense and Sensibility,* p. 8.

p. 78 Austen, "an absolute old bachelor . . ." is from J. Austen, *Sense and Sensibility,* p. 28.

p. 78 Marianne Dashwood [Austen], "He talked of flannel waistcoats . . ." is from J. Austen, *Sense and Sensibility,* p. 30.

p. 80 Austen, "he was the husband . . ." is from J. Austen, *Sense and Sensibility,* p. 82.

p. 80 Austen, "though her complexion varied . . ." is from J. Austen, *Sense and Sensibility,* p. 94.

p. 83 Austen, "was born to discover . . ." is from J. Austen, *Sense and Sensibility,* p. 268.

p. 83 Manservant [Austen], "Mr. Ferrars is married," is from J. Austen, *Sense and Sensibility,* p. 250.

p. 84 Austen, "he fled from society . . ." is from J. Austen, *Sense and Sensibility,* p. 268.

p. 84 "intimate knowledge of life . . ." is from an untitled review of *Sense and Sensibility, British Critic,* May 1812, p. 527.

p. 84 "is well written . . ." is from Southam 1968, p. 35.

p. 84 Countess of Bessborough, "It is a clever Novel . . ." is from Castalia, p. 418.

p. 84 Princess Charlotte, "'*Sence and Sencibility*' . . ." is from Aspinall, p. 26.

p. 85 Austen, "Marianne Dashwood was born . . ." is from J. Austen, *Sense and Sensibility,* p. 267.

Six: Light, Bright, and Sparkling

p. 87 Mary Bennet [Austen], "Pride relates more to our opinion . . ." is from J. Austen, *Pride and Prejudice,* p. 14.

p. 87 Austen, "It is a truth . . ." is from J. Austen, *Pride and Prejudice,* p. 3.

p. 88 Austen, "the business of her life," is from J. Austen, *Pride and Prejudice,* p. 4.

p. 88 Darcy [Austen], "tolerable; but not handsome . . ." is from J. Austen, *Pride and Prejudice,* p. 9.

p. 88 Austen, "rendered uncommonly intelligent . . ." is from J. Austen, *Pride and Prejudice,* p. 16.

p. 88 "Elizabeth has a thousand faults . . ." is from "Reputations Reconsidered: Jane Austen," p. 263.

p. 88 Elizabeth Bennet [Austen], "People themselves alter so much . . ." is from J. Austen, *Pride and Prejudice,* p. 30.

p. 88 Austen, "I must confess . . ." is from Le Faye 1995, p. 201.

p. 91 Collins [Austen], "It is usual with young ladies . . ." is from J. Austen, *Pride and Prejudice,* p. 73.

p. 91 Elizabeth Bennet [Austen], "Can I speak plainer?" is from J. Austen, *Pride and Prejudice,* p. 74.

p. 92 Darcy [Austen], "a most unhappy connection," is from J. Austen, *Pride and Prejudice,* p. 131.

p. 92 Darcy [Austen], "the total want of propriety," is from J. Austen, *Pride and Prejudice,* p. 130.

p. 94 Elizabeth Bennet [Austen], "How despicably I have acted . . ." and "Till this moment . . ." are from J. Austen, *Pride and Prejudice,* p. 137.

p. 94 Austen, "to be mistress of Pemberley . . ." is from J. Austen, *Pride and Prejudice,* p. 159.

p. 96 Austen, "She began now to comprehend . . ." is from J. Austen, *Pride and Prejudice,* p. 202.

p. 96 de Bourgh [Austen], "the upstart pretensions . . ." is from J. Austen, *Pride and Prejudice,* p. 232.

p. 96 Elizabeth Bennet [Austen], "He is a gentleman . . ." is from J. Austen, *Pride and Prejudice,* p. 232.

p. 96 de Bourgh [Austen], "True. You *are* a gentleman's daughter . . ." is from J. Austen, *Pride and Prejudice,* p. 232.

p. 96 Darcy [Austen], "*My* affections and wishes . . ." is from J. Austen, *Pride and Prejudice,* p. 239.

p. 97 Austen, "gave him to understand . . ." is from J. Austen, *Pride and Prejudice,* p. 239.

p. 98 "By the Author of *Sense and Sensibility,*" is quoted in Tomalin, p. 221.

p. 98 "very far superior . . ." and "excites the interest," and "sense and conduct . . ." are quoted in Halperin, p. 210.

p. 98 Austen, "The work is rather too light . . ." is from Le Faye 1995, p. 203.

p. 98 Fanny Knight, "[Aunt Jane] & I . . ." is quoted in Tomalin, p. 239.

p. 99 Austen, "The Secret has spread so far . . ." is from Le Faye 1995, p. 231.

p. 99 Mitford, "Wickham is equally bad . . ." is from L'Estrange, p. 300.

p. 99 Twain, "Every time I read . . ." is quoted in Southam 1987, p. 232.

p. 99 Twain, "the thing involved . . ." and "that there are fine things . . ." are quoted in Auerbach.

p. 100 Henry Austen, "a woman of brilliant generous and cultivated mind . . ." is quoted in Le Faye 2002, p. 172.

p. 101 Austen, "exactly herself . . ." is from Chapman 1952, p. 310.

p. 101 Austen, "I can only imagine . . ." is from Woolsey, p. 193.

p. 101 Austen, "Mrs. F. is not careful enough . . ." and "You are but *now* coming . . ." are from Chapman 1952, p. 401.

p. 102 Austen, "not to think of accepting . . ." is from Chapman 1952, p. 410.

Seven: Vice and Virtue

p. 103 Austen, "What strange creatures . . ." is from Chapman 1952, p. 408.

p. 105 Austen, "Poor Woman . . ." is from Le Faye 1995, p. 208.

p. 105 Princess Charlotte, "Heaven defend any poor girl . . ." is quoted in Richardson, p. 90.

p. 106 Mrs. Norris [Austen], "Wherever you are . . ." is from J. Austen, *Mansfield Park,* pp. 151–152.

p. 106 Austen, "young people of fortune," and "vicious conduct," are from J. Austen, *Mansfield Park,* p. 30.

p. 107 Mary Crawford [Austen], "Be honest and poor . . ." is from J. Austen, *Mansfield Park,* p. 147.

p. 107 Austen, "Children of the same family . . ." is from J. Austen, *Mansfield Park,* p. 161.

p. 108 Mary Crawford [Austen], "Fanny Price! Nonsense . . ." is from J. Austen, *Mansfield Park,* p. 157.

p. 108 Henry Crawford [Austen], "But I cannot be satisfied . . ." is from J. Austen, *Mansfield Park,* p. 157.

p. 108 Austen, "how wretched . . ." is from J. Austen, *Mansfield Park,* p. 220.

p. 112 "*Mansfield Park* is altogether an old book . . ." is from Bloom 2008, p. 150.

p. 112 Mitford, "stiffened into the most perpendicular . . ." is from Mitford, p. 127.

p. 112 Henry Austen, "Her voice was extremely sweet . . ." is quoted in Southam, p. 83.

p. 112 Cassandra Austen, "Fond of Fanny" and the other opinions of *Mansfield Park* are from Chapman 1980, pp. 432–435.

p. 115 Austen, "Emma, Dedicated by Permission . . ." is quoted in Tomalin, p. 249.

p. 115 Austen [Murray], "To His Royal Highness . . ." is from J. Austen, *Emma,* frontispiece.

p. 115 Clarke, "The Habits of Life and Character . . ." is from Chapman 1952, p. 430.

p. 116 Austen, "Such a man's conversation . . ." is from Chapman 1952, p. 443.

p. 116 Clarke, "Do let us have an English Clergyman . . ." is from Chapman 1952, pp. 444–445.

p. 116 Austen, "The most excellent Man . . ." and other quotations from "Plan of a Novel" are from Chapman 1980, pp. 428–430.

Eight: "If I Live to Be an Old Woman . . ."

p. 118 Austen, "There are so many . . ." is from J. Austen, *Persuasion,* p. 103.

p. 118 Austen, "The real evils . . ." is from J. Austen, *Emma,* p. 1.

p. 119 Austen, "the stain of illegitimacy," is from J. Austen, *Emma,* p. 317.

p. 121 Austen, "in possession of an independent fortune . . ." is from J. Austen, *Emma,* p. 117.

p. 121 Mrs. Elton [Austen], "How do you like . . ." is from J. Austen, *Emma,* p. 211.

p. 121 Austen, "youth had passed . . ." is from J. Austen, *Emma,* p. 12.

p. 123 Austen, "Never had she felt . . ." is from J. Austen, *Emma,* p. 246.

p. 123 Austen, "Emma felt the tears . . ." is from J. Austen, *Emma,* pp. 246–247.

p. 124 Austen, "Till now that she was threatened . . ." is from J. Austen, *Emma,* p. 272.

p. 124 Austen, "What did she say . . ." is from J. Austen, *Emma,* p. 283.

p. 124 Mrs. Austen, "more entertaining . . ." and the other opinions of *Emma* are from Chapman 1980, pp. 436–439.

p. 126 Scott, "the author displays her peculiar powers . . ." is from Scott, p. 196.

p. 126 Scott, "to the reader . . ." is from Scott, p. 193.

p. 126 Trollope, "very tedious . . ." is from Ferguson, p. 461.

p. 127 Austen, "Miss Catherine . . ." and "I hope Heaven . . ." are from Le Faye 1995, p. 333.

p. 128 Caroline Austen, "My uncle had been living . . ." is from Caroline Austen, p. 48.

p. 129 Austen, "Composition seems to me . . ." is from Le Faye 1995, p. 321.

p. 129 Austen, "stronger than I was . . ." from Le Faye 1995, p. 326.

p. 130 Austen, "just a little pain . . ." from Le Faye 1995, p. 329.

p. 130 Caroline Austen, "never looked comfortable . . ." is quoted in Tomalin, p. 263.

p. 131 Caroline Austen, "quite like an invalide . . ." is quoted in Tomalin, p. 265.

p. 132 Austen, "gradually removed the Evil," from Le Faye 1995, p. 340.

p. 132 Austen, "to my dearest Sister . . ." is from Jane Austen's will, which is in the collections of the National Archives of Great Britain.

p. 132 Austen, "Now, that's the sort of thing . . ." from Le Faye 1995, pp. 340–341.

p. 132 Austen, "If I live to be . . ." from Le Faye 1995, p. 341.

p. 135 Mary Austen, "stay'd with Jane . . . ," "Jane Austen worse . . . ," and "Jane in great danger . . ." are quoted in Tomalin, p. 268.

p. 135 James Austen, "We can no longer flatter ourselves . . ." is from Tucker, p. 111.

Nine: Lasting Words

p. 136 Austen, "There is no charm equal . . ." is from J. Austen, *Emma,* p. 174.

p. 136 Austen, "These races & revels . . ." is from Chapman 1980, p. 452.

p. 137 Mary Austen, "Jane breathed her last . . ." and Cassandra Austen, "She was the sun . . ." are quoted in Tomalin, p. 272.

p. 137 James Austen, "In her (rare union) . . ." is from Selwyn, p. 257.

p. 138 Henry Austen, "the benevolence of her heart . . ." is quoted in Halperin, p. 8.

p. 139 Austen, "not in the least . . ." and "as anybody might expect," are from J. Austen, *Northanger Abbey,* p. 5.

p. 139 Austen, "Almost pretty," is from J. Austen, *Northanger Abbey,* p. 6.

p. 139 Austen, "a very gentleman-like" is from J. Austen, *Northanger Abbey,* p. 14.

p. 140 John Thorpe [Austen], "the finest girl in Bath," is from J. Austen, *Northanger Abbey,* p. 65.

p. 140 Catherine Morland [Austen], "a fine old place . . ." is from J. Austen, *Northanger Abbey,* p. 107.

p. 142 Austen, "the blackest suspicions," is from J. Austen, *Northanger Abbey,* p. 128.

p. 142 Henry Tilney [Austen], "Dear Miss Morland . . ." is from J. Austen, *Northanger Abbey,* p. 136.

p. 142 Austen, "The visions of romance . . ." is from J. Austen, *Northanger Abbey,* p. 136.

p. 143 Austen, "a man of fortune . . ." is from J. Austen, *Northanger Abbey,* p. 172.

p. 143 General Tilney [Austen], "to be a fool . . ." is from J. Austen, *Northanger Abbey,* p. 172.

p. 143 Austen, "There seems almost a general wish . . ." is from J. Austen, *Northanger Abbey,* pp. 22–23.

p. 145 Austen, "feeling himself ill-used . . ." is from J. Austen, *Persuasion,* p. 19.

p. 145 Austen, "attachment and regrets . . ." is from J. Austen, *Persuasion,* pp. 19–20.

p. 145 Austen, "was nobody with either father or sister . . ." is from J. Austen, *Persuasion,* p. 5.

p. 148 Anne Elliot [Austen], "All the privilege I claim . . ." is from J. Austen, *Persuasion,* p. 157.

p. 148 Frederick Wentworth [Austen], "Dare not say that man forgets . . ." is from J. Austen, *Persuasion,* p. 158.

p. 148 Austen, "When any two young people . . ." and "maturity of mind . . ." are from J. Austen, *Persuasion,* p. 165.

p. 148 Austen, "dread of a future war . . ." is from J. Austen, *Persuasion,* p. 168.

p. 148 Austen, "How eloquent could Anne Elliot have been . . ." is from J. Austen, *Persuasion,* p. 21.

p. 150 Cassandra Austen, "Dear, dear Jane . . ." is quoted in Chapman 1937, p. 116.

Afterword

p. 151 Austen, "The person, be it gentleman or lady . . ." is from J. Austen, *Northanger Abbey,* p. 72.

p. 152 Austen-Leigh, "However little I may have to tell . . ." is from James Edward Austen-Leigh, p. 3.

p. 152 "She has ceased to be . . ." is from Bailey, p. 30.

p. 152 Kipling, "There's no one to touch Jane . . ." is from Kipling, p. 752.

p. 155 Maugham, "Nothing very much happens . . ." is from Maugham, p. 67.

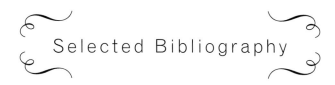

Selected Bibliography

Aspinall, A., ed. *Letters of the Princess Charlotte, 1811–1817.* London: Home and Van Thal, 1949.

Auerbach, Emily. "'A Barkeeper Entering the Kingdom of Heaven': Did Mark Twain Really Hate Jane Austen?" *Virginia Quarterly Review,* winter 1999. Available online. URL: www.vqronline.org/articles/1999/winter/auerbach-barkeeper-entering/. Downloaded on April 26, 2010.

Austen, Caroline. *Reminiscences of Caroline Austen.* N.p.: Jane Austen Society, 1986.

Austen, Henry. "Biographical Notice of the Author." In *Northanger Abbey and Persuasion,* by Jane Austen. London: John Murray, 1818.

Austen, Jane. *Catharine and Other Writings.* New York: Oxford University Press, 1993.

__________. *Emma.* New York: W. W. Norton and Co., 2000.

__________. *Mansfield Park.* New York: W. W. Norton and Co., 1998.

__________. *Northanger Abbey.* New York: W. W. Norton and Co., 2004.

__________. *Persuasion.* New York: W. W. Norton and Co., 1995.

__________. *Pride and Prejudice.* New York: W. W. Norton and Co., 2001.

__________. *Sense and Sensibility.* New York: W. W. Norton and Co., 2002.

__________. *The Watsons,* in *Northanger Abbey; Lady Susan; The Watsons; Sanditon.* Oxford, U.K.: Oxford University Press, 2003.

Austen-Leigh, James Edward. *A Memoir of Jane Austen.* London: R. Bentley and Son, 1872.

Austen-Leigh, Richard A. *Pedigree of Austen; Austen Papers, 1704–1856.* London: Routledge/Thoemmes Press, 1995.

Austen-Leigh, William, and Richard Arthur Austen-Leigh. *Jane Austen: A Family Record.* Boston: G. K. Hall and Co., 1989.

__________. *Jane Austen, Her Life and Letters: A Family Record.* London: John Murray, 1913.

Bailey, John. *Introductions to Jane Austen.* London: Oxford University Press, 1931.

Beer, Frances, ed. *The Juvenilia of Jane Austen and Charlotte Brontë.* Harmondsworth, Middlesex, U.K.: Penguin Books, 1986.

Bloom, Harold. *Jane Austen.* New York: Bloom's Literary Criticism, 2008.

Bloom, Harold. *Jane Austen.* New York: Chelsea House, 1986.

Burney, Frances. *Cecilia, or Memoirs of an Heiress.* Oxford, U.K.: Oxford University Press, 2008.

Castalia, Countess Granville, ed. *Lord Granville Leveson Gower (First Earl Granville): Private Correspondence, 1781 to 1821.* Vol 2. London: John Murray, 1916.

Chapman, R. W. *Jane Austen: Facts and Problems.* Oxford, U.K.: Clarendon Press, 1949.

__________. "Jane Austen's Text: Authoritative Manuscript Corrections." *Times Literary Supplement,* February 13, 1937, p. 116.

__________, ed. *Jane Austen's Letters to Her Sister Cassandra and Others.* London: Oxford University Press, 1952.

__________, ed. *The Novels of Jane Austen.* Vol. 6: *Minor Works.* London: Oxford University Press, 1980.

Elwood, Anne Katharine. *Memoirs of the Literary Ladies of England, from the Commencement of the Last Century.* Vol. 2. London: Henry Colburn, 1843.

Ferguson, Frances, ed. *Jane Austen's* Emma. New York: Pearson/Longman, 2006.

Francklin, Thomas. *Matilda: A Tragedy.* London: T. Cadell, 1775.

The Habits of Good Society: A Handbook for Ladies and Gentlemen. New York: Carleton, 1869.

Halperin, John. *The Life of Jane Austen.* Baltimore: Johns Hopkins University Press, 1996.

Hopkins, Donald R. *Princes and Peasants: Smallpox in History.* Chicago: University of Chicago Press, 1983.

Kipling, Rudyard. *Collected Stories.* New York: Everyman's Library, 1994.

Le Faye, D. G. "Recollections of Chawton." *Times Literary Supplement,* May 3, 1985, p. 495.

Le Faye, Deirdre. "Anna Lefroy's Original Memories of Jane Austen." *Review of English Studies,* August 1988, pp. 417–421.

__________. "Jane Austen and Her Hancock Relatives." *Review of English Studies,* February 1979, pp. 12–27.

__________. *Jane Austen's "Outlandish Cousin."* London: British Library, 2002.

__________, ed. *Jane Austen's Letters.* Oxford, U.K.: Oxford University Press, 1995.

L'Estrange, A. G., ed. *The Life of Mary Russell Mitford.* Vol. 1. London: Richard Bentley, 1870.

"Letters to the Editor: Jane Austen." *Times Literary Supplement*, September 15, 1954, p. 591.

Mack, Robert L., ed. *The Loiterer.* Lewiston, N.Y.: Edwin Mellen Press, 2006.

Maugham, W. Somerset. *Ten Novels and Their Authors.* London: William Heinemann, 1954.

Mitford, Mary Russell. *The Letters of Mary Russell Mitford.* Port Washington, N.Y.: Kennikat Press, 1972.

Nokes, David. *Jane Austen: A Life.* New York: Farrar, Straus and Giroux, 1997.

Norman, Andrew. *Jane Austen: An Unrequited Love.* Stroud, Gloucestershire, U.K.: History Press, 2009.

"Reputations Reconsidered: Jane Austen." *The Academy,* March 5, 1898, pp. 262–264.

Richardson, Joanna. "The Princess Charlotte." *History Today,* February 1972, pp. 87–93.

Scott, Walter. "Emma; a Novel. By the Author of Sense and Sensibility, Pride and Prejudice, &c." *Quarterly Review,* October 1815, pp. 188–201.

Selwyn, David, ed. *Collected Poems and Verse of the Austen Family.* Manchester, U.K.: Carcanet Press, 1996.

Southam, B.C., ed. *Jane Austen: The Critical Heritage,* Vol. 1. London: Routledge and K. Paul, 1968.

__________. *Jane Austen: The Critical Heritage,* Vol. 2. London: Routledge and K. Paul, 1987.

Swift, Jonathan. *The Works of Dean Swift.* New York: Derby and Jackson, 1857.

Tomalin, Claire. *Jane Austen: A Life.* New York: Vintage Books, 1999.

Tucker, George Holbert. *A Goodly Heritage: A History of Jane Austen's Family.* Manchester, U.K.: Carcanet New Press, 1983.

Untitled review of *Sense and Sensibility. British Critic,* May 1812, p. 527.

"*Vanity Fair*—and *Jane Eyre.*" *Quarterly Review,* December 1848 and March 1849, pp. 153–185.

Wollstonecraft, Mary. *A Vindication of the Rights of Woman: With Strictures on Political and Moral Subjects.* London: J. Johnson, 1792.

Woolsey, Sarah Chauncey, ed. *The Letters of Jane Austen.* Boston: Roberts Brothers, 1892.

Jane Austen's Works

Jane Austen is known best for her six novels, which were published anonymously between 1811 and 1818. She also wrote stories, plays, poems, satires, and letters that she never intended to publish, and she began two novels that she never finished. After Austen was recognized as one of the world's great novelists, all her writing found its way into print.

THE SIX COMPLETED NOVELS

Today's readers can choose from many editions of Austen's novels, but these were the first.

Sense and Sensibility. London: Thomas Egerton, 1811.
Pride and Prejudice. London: Thomas Egerton, 1813.
Mansfield Park. London: Thomas Egerton, 1814.
Emma. London: John Murray, 1816 (released in December 1815).
Northanger Abbey and *Persuasion.* London: John Murray, 1818 (released in December 1817).

THE UNFINISHED NOVELS

These two works were published most recently in a single volume.

Sanditon & The Watsons. Mineola, N.Y.: Dover Publications, 2007.

THE WRITING OF JANE AUSTEN'S YOUTH

Juvenilia. Cambridge, U.K.: Cambridge University Press, 2006.

Lady Susan. New York: Garland Publishing, 1989.

POETRY

The Poetry of Jane Austen and the Austen Family, edited by David Selwyn. Iowa City: University of Iowa Press, 1997.

LETTERS

This is the most recent complete edition of Austen's correspondence.

Jane Austen's Letters, edited by Deirdre Le Faye. Oxford, U.K.: Oxford University Press, 1995.

Picture Credits

With permission from the Provost and Scholars of King's College, Cambridge: 2

© National Portrait Gallery, London: 4, 34, 40

Library of Congress: 6, 9, 13, 36, 48, 52, 58, 59, 61, 77, 79, 81, 89, 90, 100, 105, 111, 120, 138, 140, 141, 142, 144, 149

Photofest: 8, 82, 93, 109, 125, 146, 154

T06734 by The Tate Gallery/Digital Image © Tate, London 2009 *Portrait of Sir Francis Ford's Children Giving a Coin to a Beggar Boy,* Sir William Beechey, 1753–1839: 16

Knight Family Collection, Chawton House Library (www.chawton-house.org): 19

Museum of London: 20

Jane Austen Memorial Trust: 14, 23, 31, 44, 45, 62, 95, 113, 126, 128, 130

The British Library Board shelfmark Add 59874, f, 8JV-86; 1267.f.21, plate 3: 29, 51

The Pierpont Morgan Library/Art Resource, NY: 56, 75

National Library of Medicine: 68

The University of Southampton: 71

Print Collection, Miriam and Ira D. Wallach Division of Art, Prints and Photographs, The New York Public Library, Astor, Lenox and Tilden Foundations: 85

The National Archives of Great Britain: 133

Index

Note: Page numbers in *italics* refer to illustrations.

Catherine Reef is the author of more than forty nonfiction books for young people and adults, many of them award winners. Her previous Clarion biographies of writers include the highly acclaimed *Ernest Hemingway: A Writer's Life* and *E. E. Cummings: A Poet's Life*. She lives in College Park, Maryland.